LET'S LEARN

絵とき辞書で日本語を学びましょう

JAPANESE

PICTURE DICTIONARY

By
The Editors of
Passport Books

Illustrated by
Marlene Goodman

McGraw·Hill

New York   Chicago   San Francisco   Lisbon   London   Madrid   Mexico City
Milan   New Delhi   San Juan   Seoul   Singapore   Sydney   Toronto

Welcome to the *Let's Learn Japanese* Picture Dictionary!

Here's an exciting way for you to learn more than 1,500 words that will help you speak about many of your favorite subjects. With these words, you will be able to talk about your house, sports, outer space, the ocean, and many more subjects.

This dictionary is fun to use. On each page, you will see drawings with the words that describe them underneath. These drawings are usually part of a large, colorful scene. See if you can find all the words in the big scene! You will enjoy looking at the pictures more and more as you learn new words.

At the back of the book, you will find a Japanese-English Glossary and Index and an English-Japanese Glossary and Index, where you can look up words in alphabetical order, and find out exactly where the words are located in the dictionary.

This is a book you can look at over and over again, and each time you look, you will find something new. You'll be able to talk about people, places, and things you know, and you'll learn lots of new words as you go along!

The McGraw-Hill Companies

Illustrations by Terrie Meider
7. Clothing; 15. People in Our Community; 18. Sports; 28. Colors;
29. The Family Tree; 30. Shapes; 31. Numbers; 32. Map of the World

3 4 5 6 7 8 9 0   WKT/WKT   1 0 9 8 7 6 5 4

ISBN 0-07-140827-4

McGraw-Hill books are available at special quantity discounts to use as premiums and sales promotions, or for use in corporate training programs. For more information, please write to the Director of Special Sales, Professional Publishing, McGraw-Hill, Two Penn Plaza, New York, NY 10121-2298. Or contact your local bookstore.

This book is printed on acid-free paper.

Table of Contents   mokuji   目　次

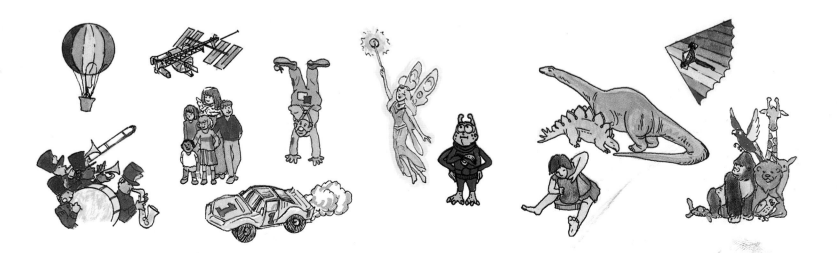

1. Our Classroom　kyōshitsu　教室

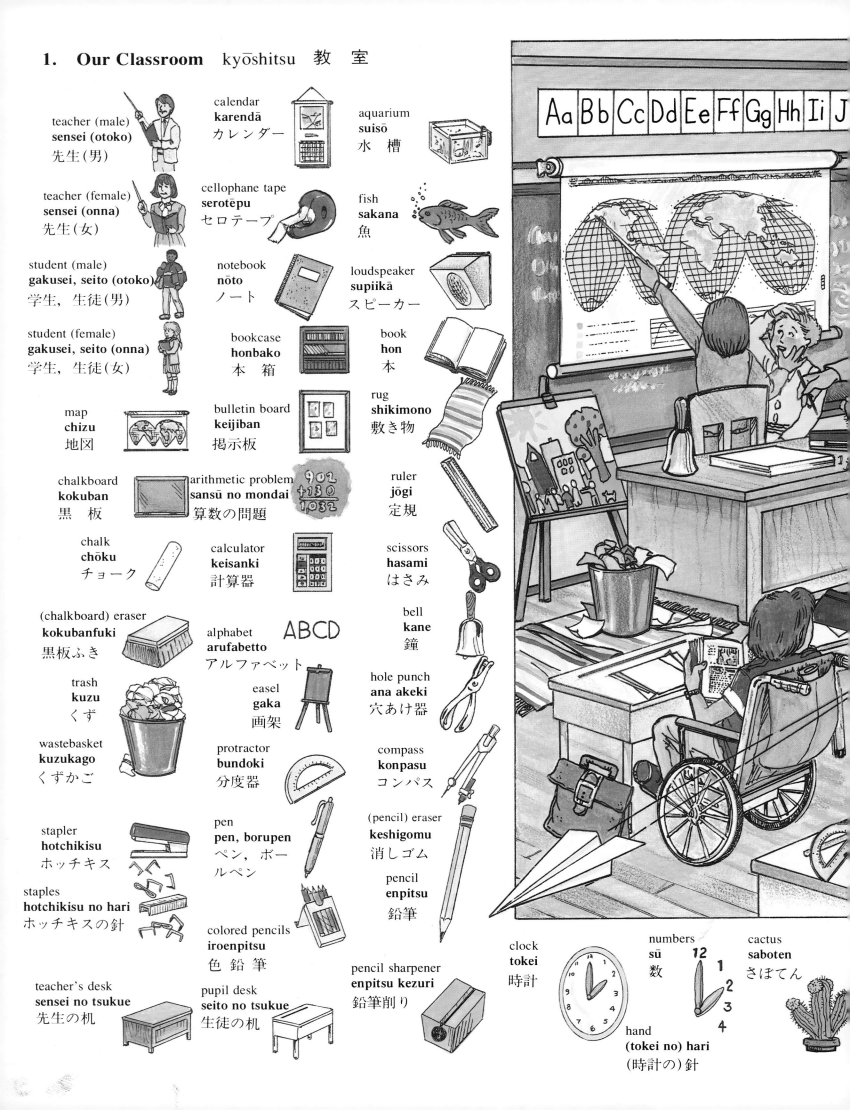

teacher (male)
sensei (otoko)
先生（男）

teacher (female)
sensei (onna)
先生（女）

student (male)
gakusei, seito (otoko)
学生，生徒（男）

student (female)
gakusei, seito (onna)
学生，生徒（女）

map
chizu
地図

chalkboard
kokuban
黒板

chalk
chōku
チョーク

(chalkboard) eraser
kokubanfuki
黒板ふき

trash
kuzu
くず

wastebasket
kuzukago
くずかご

stapler
hotchikisu
ホッチキス

staples
hotchikisu no hari
ホッチキスの針

teacher's desk
sensei no tsukue
先生の机

calendar
karendā
カレンダー

cellophane tape
serotēpu
セロテープ

notebook
nōto
ノート

bookcase
honbako
本箱

bulletin board
keijiban
掲示板

arithmetic problem
sansū no mondai
算数の問題

calculator
keisanki
計算器

alphabet
arufabetto
アルファベット

ABCD

easel
gaka
画架

protractor
bundoki
分度器

pen
pen, borupen
ペン，ボールペン

colored pencils
iroenpitsu
色鉛筆

pupil desk
seito no tsukue
生徒の机

aquarium
suisō
水槽

fish
sakana
魚

loudspeaker
supiikā
スピーカー

book
hon
本

rug
shikimono
敷き物

ruler
jōgi
定規

scissors
hasami
はさみ

bell
kane
鐘

hole punch
ana akeki
穴あけ器

compass
konpasu
コンパス

(pencil) eraser
keshigomu
消しゴム

pencil
enpitsu
鉛筆

pencil sharpener
enpitsu kezuri
鉛筆削り

clock
tokei
時計

numbers
sū
数

hand
(tokei no) hari
（時計の）針

cactus
saboten
さぼてん

plant
shokubutsu
植物

glue
setchakuzai
接着剤

globe
chikyūgi
地球儀

picture
e
絵

paint
enogu
絵の具

paintbrush
efude
絵筆

paper
kami
紙

crayon
kureyon
クレヨン

2. Our House   ie, jūtaku 家，住宅

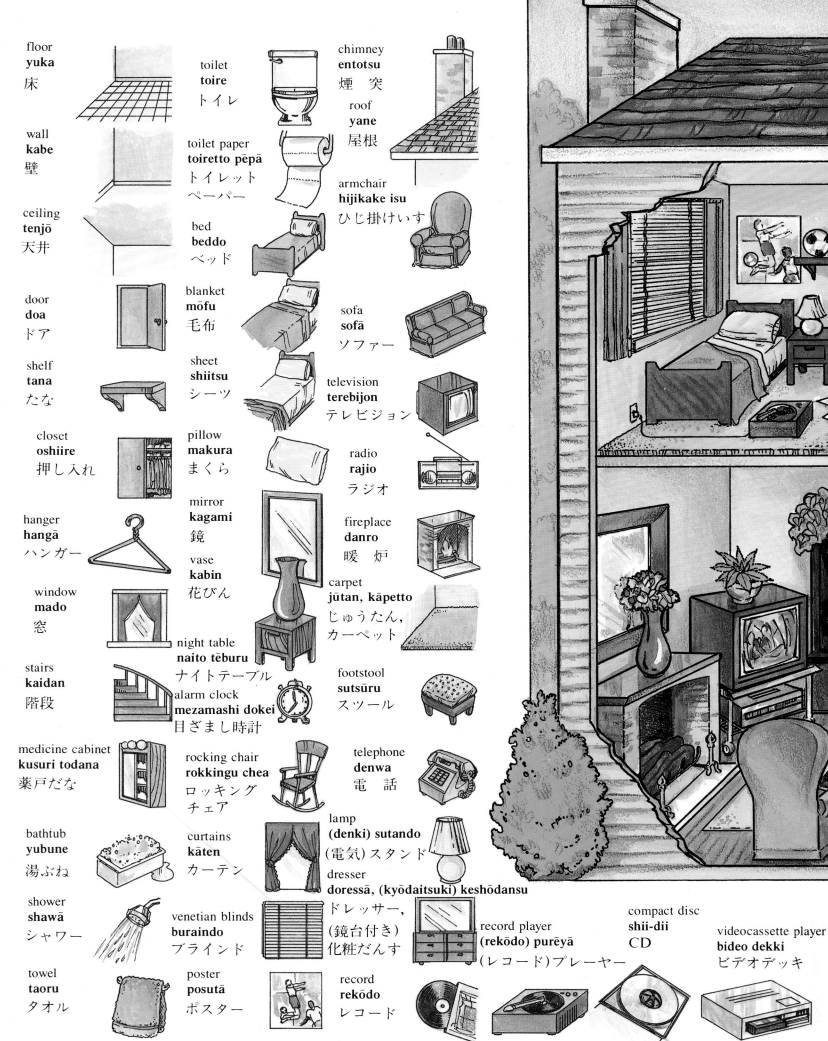

floor
yuka
床

wall
kabe
壁

ceiling
tenjō
天井

door
doa
ドア

shelf
tana
たな

closet
oshiire
押し入れ

hanger
hangā
ハンガー

window
mado
窓

stairs
kaidan
階段

medicine cabinet
kusuri todana
薬戸だな

bathtub
yubune
湯ぶね

shower
shawā
シャワー

towel
taoru
タオル

toilet
toire
トイレ

toilet paper
toiretto pēpā
トイレット
ペーパー

bed
beddo
ベッド

blanket
mōfu
毛布

sheet
shiitsu
シーツ

pillow
makura
まくら

mirror
kagami
鏡

vase
kabin
花びん

night table
naito tēburu
ナイトテーブル

alarm clock
mezamashi dokei
目ざまし時計

rocking chair
rokkingu chea
ロッキング
チェア

curtains
kāten
カーテン

venetian blinds
buraindo
ブラインド

poster
posutā
ポスター

chimney
entotsu
煙突

roof
yane
屋根

armchair
hijikake isu
ひじ掛けいす

sofa
sofā
ソファー

television
terebijon
テレビジョン

radio
rajio
ラジオ

fireplace
danro
暖炉

carpet
jūtan, kāpetto
じゅうたん，
カーペット

footstool
sutsūru
スツール

telephone
denwa
電話

lamp
(denki) sutando
(電気)スタンド

dresser
doressā, (kyōdaitsuki) keshōdansu
ドレッサー，
(鏡台付き)
化粧だんす

record player
(rekōdo) purēyā
(レコード)プレーヤー

record
rekōdo
レコード

compact disc
shii-dii
CD

videocassette player
bideo dekki
ビデオデッキ

bedroom
shinshitsu
寝 室

bathroom
yokushitsu
浴 室

living room
ima
居 間

dining room
dainingu rūmu
ダイニングルーム

kitchen
daidokoro
台 所

cassette tape
kasetto tēpu
カセットテープ

cassette player
kasetto dekki
カセットデッキ

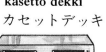

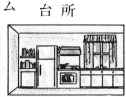

3. The Kitchen daidokoro 台所

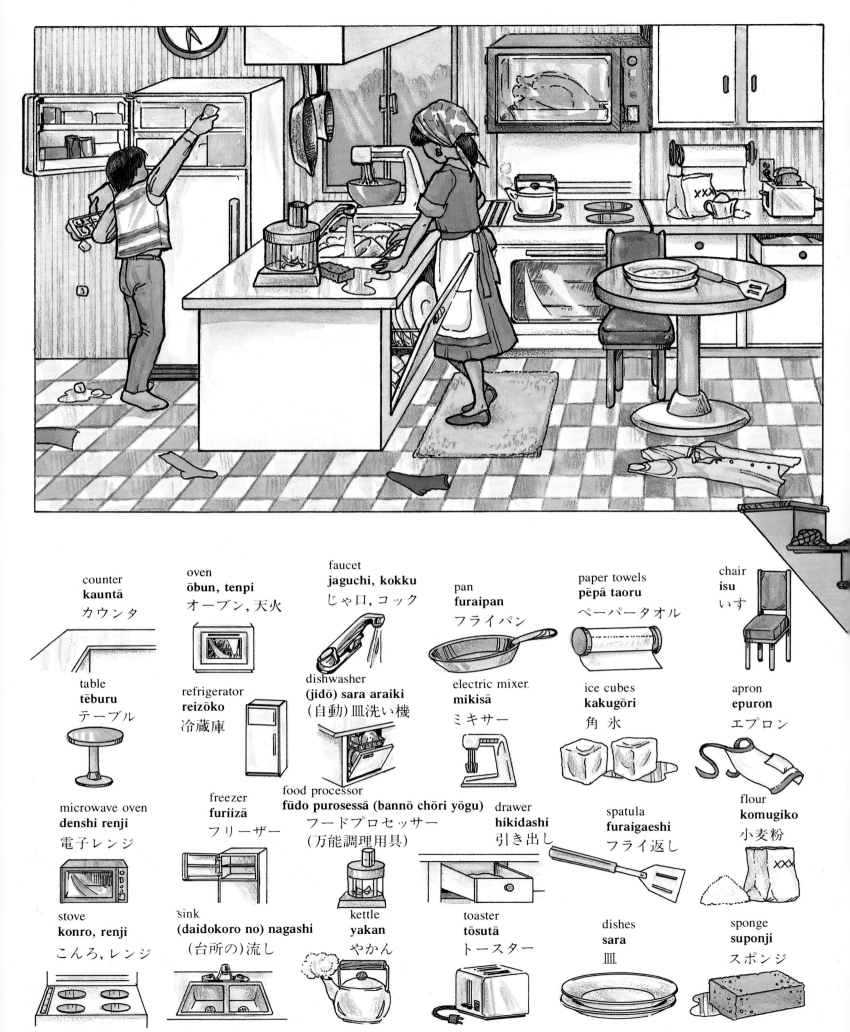

counter
kauntā
カウンタ

oven
ōbun, tenpi
オーブン, 天火

faucet
jaguchi, kokku
じゃ口, コック

pan
furaipan
フライパン

paper towels
pēpā taoru
ペーパータオル

chair
isu
いす

table
tēburu
テーブル

refrigerator
reizōko
冷蔵庫

dishwasher
(jidō) sara araiki
(自動) 皿洗い機

electric mixer
mikisā
ミキサー

ice cubes
kakugōri
角 氷

apron
epuron
エプロン

microwave oven
denshi renji
電子レンジ

freezer
furiizā
フリーザー

food processor
fūdo purosessā (bannō chōri yōgu)
フードプロセッサー
(万能調理用具)

drawer
hikidashi
引き出し

spatula
furaigaeshi
フライ返し

flour
komugiko
小麦粉

stove
konro, renji
こんろ, レンジ

sink
(daidokoro no) nagashi
(台所の) 流し

kettle
yakan
やかん

toaster
tōsutā
トースター

dishes
sara
皿

sponge
suponji
スポンジ

washing machine
sentakuki
洗たく機

iron
airon
アイロン

screw
neji
ねじ

toolbox
dōgubako
道具箱

laundry detergent
senzai
洗　剤

laundry
sentakumono
洗たく物

broom
hōki
ほうき

mop
moppu
モップ

screwdriver
nejimawashi
ねじ回し

wrench
supanā, renchi
スパナー, レンチ

wood
mokuzai
木材

board
ita
板

vacuum cleaner
denki sōjiki
電気そうじ機

dustpan
chiritori
ちり取り

drill
doriru
ドリル

electrical outlet
konsento
コンセント

sandpaper
kamiyasuri
紙やすり

flashlight
kaichū dentō
懐中電燈

ironing board
airondai
アイロン台

hammer
kanazuchi
金づち

nail
kugi
くぎ

file
yasuri
やすり

brick
renga
れんが

tape measure
makijaku
巻き尺

saw
nokogiri
のこぎり

clothes dryer
(sentakumono no) kansōki
(洗たく物の) 乾燥器

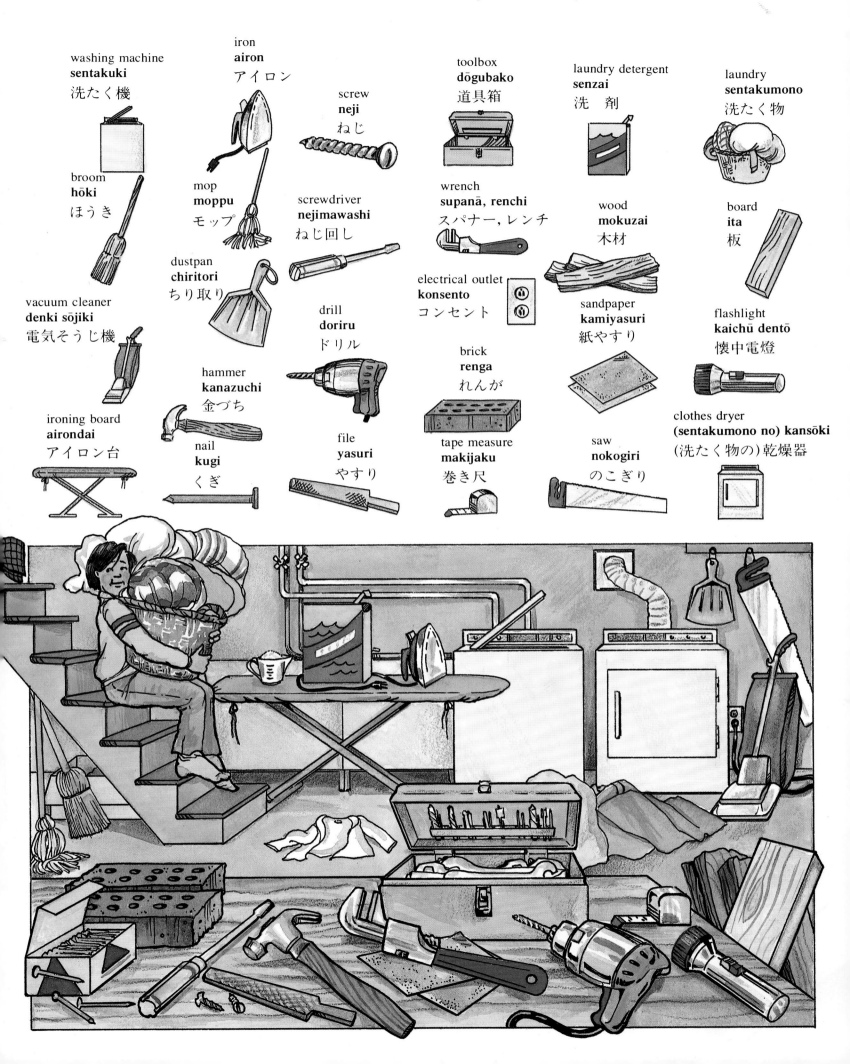

4. The Attic   yaneura beya   屋根裏部屋

trunk
toranku
トランク

box
hako
箱

dust
hokori, chiri
ほこり, ちり

string
himo, ito
ひも, 糸

cobweb
kumo no su
くもの巣

ball gown
butōkaiyō doresu
舞踏会用ドレス

top hat
shiruku hatto
シルクハット

tuxedo
takishiido
タキシード

hat
bōshi
帽子

feather
hane
羽

cowboy hat
kaubōi hatto
カウボーイ
ハット

uniform
yunihōmu
ユニホーム

cowboy boots
kaubōi būtsu
カウボーイブーツ

photo album
arubamu
アルバム

game
gēmu, gēmuban
ゲーム,
ゲーム盤

doll
ningyō
人形

jigsaw puzzle
jigusō pazuru
ジグソーパズル

jump rope
tobinawa
飛びなわ

teddy bear
kuma no nuigurumi
クマの縫い
ぐるみ

toys
omocha
おもちゃ

whistle
fue
笛

cards
toranpu
トランプ

dice
saikoro
さいころ

blocks
tsumiki
積み木

electric train
denki kikansha
電気機関車

magnet
jishaku
磁石

cradle
yurikago
揺りかご

coloring book
nurie
ぬりえ

music box
orugōru
オルゴール

yarn
keito
毛糸

knitting needles
amibari
編み針

dollhouse
ningyō no ie
人形の家

comic books
mangabon
漫画本

lightbulb
denkyū
電球

toy soldiers
omocha no heitai
おもちゃの兵隊

movie projector
eishaki
映写機

umbrella
kasa
かさ

puppet
yubi ningyō
ゆび人形

fan
sensu
扇子

marbles
ohajiki
おはじき

rocking horse
yuri mokuba
揺り木馬

chess
chesu
チェス

photograph
shashin
写　真

spinning wheel
itoguruma, tsumugiguruma
糸車, 紡ぎ車

picture frame
gakubuchi
額　縁

rocking chair
rokkingu chea
ロッキングチェア

checkers
chekkā
チェッカー

5. The Four Seasons (Weather)   shiki (tenkō)   四季(天候)

snow
yuki
雪

sled
sori
そり

ice
kōri
氷

snowplow
josetsusha (ki)
除雪車(機)

snowflake
setsuhen
雪片

snowmobile
setsujōsha
雪上車

icicle
tsurara
つらら

snowman
yukidaruma
雪だるま

shovel
shaberu
シャベル

snowball
yuki no tama
雪の玉

snowstorm
fubuki
吹雪

log
maruta
丸太

Spring   haru   春

rain
ame
雨

flowers
hana
花

rainbow
niji
にじ

flowerbed
kadan
花壇

stem
kuki
茎

petal
hanabira
花びら

bird
tori
鳥

worm
mushi
虫

vegetable garden
katei saien
家庭菜園

raindrop
amadare
雨だれ

lightning
inazuma
いなずま

Summer natsu 夏

butterfly
chō
ちょう

fly
hae
はえ

fly swatter
haetataki
はえたたき

fan
senpūki
扇風機

sprinkler
supurinkurā
スプリン
クラー

grasshopper
batta, kirigirisu
バッタ, キリギリス

lawn mower
shibakariki
芝刈り機

barbecue
bābekyū
バーベキュー

hammock
hanmokku
ハンモック

yard
niwa
庭

deck
barukonii, rodai
バルコニー,
露台

garden hose
mizumaki hōsu
水まきホース

matches
matchi
マッチ

Fall aki 秋

wind
kaze
風

leaf
ha
葉

branch
eda
枝

fog
kiri
霧

rake
kumade
くまで

clouds
kumo
雲

kite
tako
たこ

puddle
mizutamari
水たまり

mud
doro
どろ

bird's nest
tori no su
鳥の巣

bush
kanboku
かん木

6. At the Supermarket sūpāmāketto スーパーマーケット

vegetables
yasai
野菜

cabbage
kyabetsu
キャベツ

lettuce
retasu
レタス

green beans
sayamame
さや豆

peas
endō
えんどう

carrots
ninjin
にんじん

tomatoes
tomato
トマト

potatoes
jagaimo
じゃがいも

onions
tamanegi
玉ねぎ

spinach
hōrensō
ほうれん草

avocado
abokado
アボカド

nuts
nattsu
ナッツ

chocolate
chokorēto
チョコレート

candy
kyandē
キャンデー

pie
pai
パイ

fruit
kudamono
くだもの

apple
ringo
りんご

orange
orenji
オレンジ

lemon
remon
レモン

lime
raimu
ライム

cherries
sakuranbo
さくらんぼ

banana
banana
バナナ

grapes
budō
ぶどう

strawberries
ichigo
いちご

peach
momo
桃

grapefruit
gurēpufurūtsu
グレープ
フルーツ

melon
meron
メロン

watermelon
suika
すいか

raspberries
kiichigo
きいちご

pineapple
painappuru
パイナップル

meat
niku
肉

eggs
tamago
卵

butter
batā
バター

bread
pan
パン

cheese
chiizu
チーズ

food
shokumotsu
食物

milk
gyūnyū
牛乳

cookies
kukkii
クッキー

crackers
bisuketto, kurakkā
ビスケット,
クラッカー

potato chips
poteto chippu
ポテトチップ

bottle
bin
びん

fruit juice
furūtsu jūsu
フルーツ
ジュース

cereal
**kokumotsu shoku,
shiiriaru**
穀物食, シーリアル

can
kanzume
かん詰め

frozen dinner
reitō shokuhin
冷凍食品

soap
sekken
せっけん

money
okane
お金

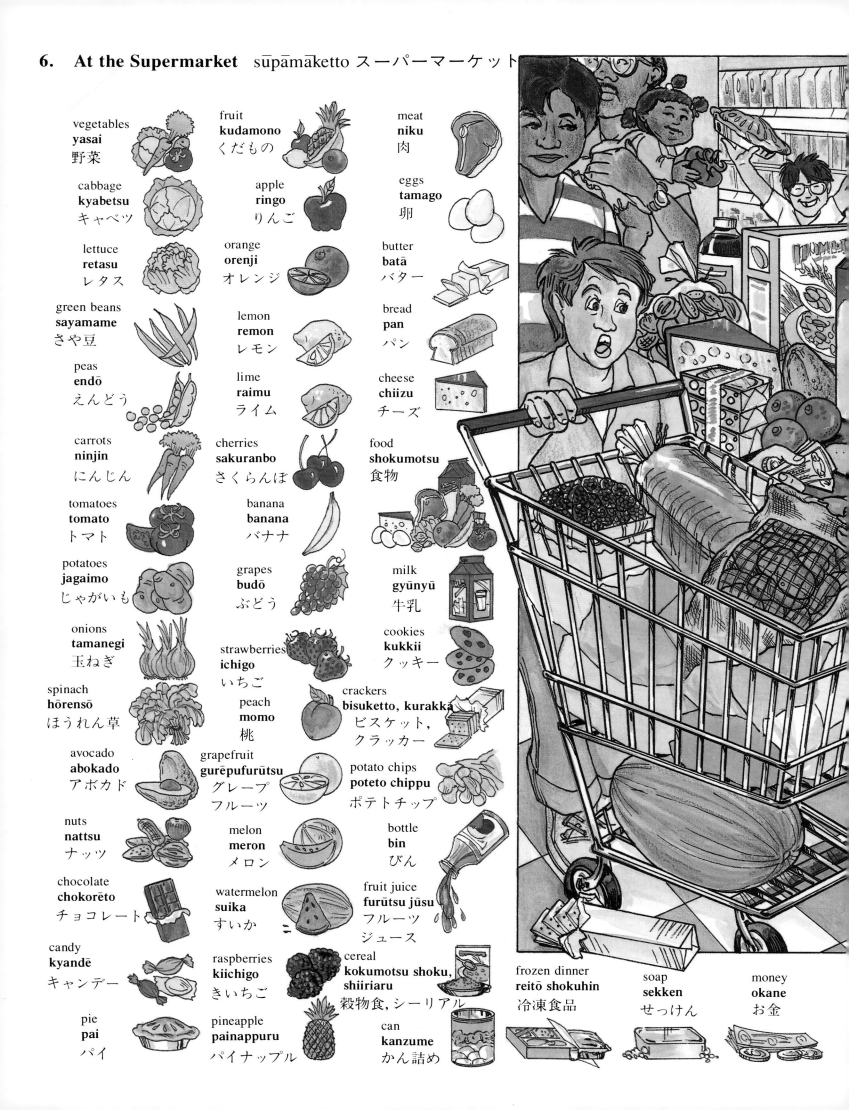

shopping cart
kaimono guruma
買い物車

shopping bag
kaimono bukuro
買い物袋

sign
hyōshiki, hyōji
標識,
表示

scale
hakari
はかり

price
nedan
値段

cash register
rejisutā
レジスター

cashier
rejisutā gakari
レジスター係

7. Clothing   mi ni tsukeru mono 身につけるもの

glasses
megane
めがね

buckle
shimegane
締め金

belt
beruto
ベルト

collar
karā, eri
カラー, えり

blouse
burausu
ブラウス

bracelet
buresuretto
ブレスレット

ring
yubiwa
指輪

skirt
sukāto
スカート

socks
sokkusu
ソックス

shoes
kutsu
くつ

underwear
shitagi
下着

pants
zubon
ズボン

tie
nekutai
ネクタイ

necklace
nekkuresu
ネックレス

sleeve
sode
そで

dress
fuku, doresu
服, ドレス

shirt
shatsu
シャツ

suit
sebiro, sūtsu
背広, スーツ

earmuffs
mimiate
耳あて

button
botan
ボタン

bathing suit
mizugi
水着

gloves
tebukuro
手袋

sweater
sētā
セーター

gym shoes
undōgutsu
運動ぐつ

shoelace
kutsuhimo
くつひも

coat
uwagi
上着

handkerchief
hankachi
ハンカチ

tights
taitsu
タイツ

hat
bōshi
帽子

sunglasses
sangurasu
サングラス

earring
iyaringu
イヤリング

shorts
hanzubon
半ズボン

sandals
sandaru
サンダル

backpack
ryukkusakku
リュックサック

down vest
chokki, besuto
チョッキ，ベスト

jeans
jiipan
ジーパン

hiking boots
haikinguyō kutsu
ハイキング用くつ

sweatshirt
torēningu shatsu
トレーニングシャツ

sweatpants
torēningu pantsu
トレーニングパンツ

t-shirt
t-shatsu
Tシャツ

watch
udedokei
腕時計

umbrella
kasa
かさ

scarf
erimaki
えり巻き

jacket
uwagi
上着

mittens
miton
ミトン

hood
fūdo
フード

raincoat
rēnkōto
レーンコート

pocket
poketto
ポケット

zipper
chakku, jippā
チャック，ジッパー

boots
būtsu
ブーツ

bathrobe
basurōbu
バスローブ

pajamas
pajama
パジャマ

cap
kyappu
キャップ

8. In the City toshi 都市

building
tatemono, biru
建物，ビル

skyscraper
chōkōsō biru
超高層ビル

factory
kōba
工場

smokestack
entotsu
煙突

traffic light
kōtsū shingōki
交通信号燈

manhole cover
manhōru no futa
マンホールのふた

driveway
shadō
車道

parking lot
chūshajō
駐車場

parking meter
pākingu mētā
パーキング
メーター

corner
magarikado,
kado, machikado
曲がりかど，
かど，町かど

fire hydrant
shōkasen
消火せん

square
hiroba
広場

statue
zō
像

apartment building
apāto
アパート

fire escape
hijō kaidan
非常階段

balcony
barukonii
バルコニー

fire station
shōbōsho
消防署

police station
keisatsusho
警察署

jail
keimusho
刑務所

bookstore
hon'ya
本屋

toy store
omochaya
おもちゃ屋

grocery story
yaoya
八百屋

bakery
pan'ya
パン屋

butcher shop
nikuya
肉屋

fountain
funsui
噴水

newspaper
shinbun
新聞

train station
(tetsudō no) eki
(鉄道の)駅

church
kyōkai
教会

school
gakkō
学校

museum
hakubutsukan
博物館

hospital
byōin
病院

drugstore
(pharmacy)
yakkyoku
薬局

movie theater
eigakan
映画館

restaurant
resutoran
レストラン

clothing store
yōfukuya
洋服屋

hotel
hoteru
ホテル

traffic jam
kōtsū jūtai
交通渋滞

crane
kurēn
クレーン

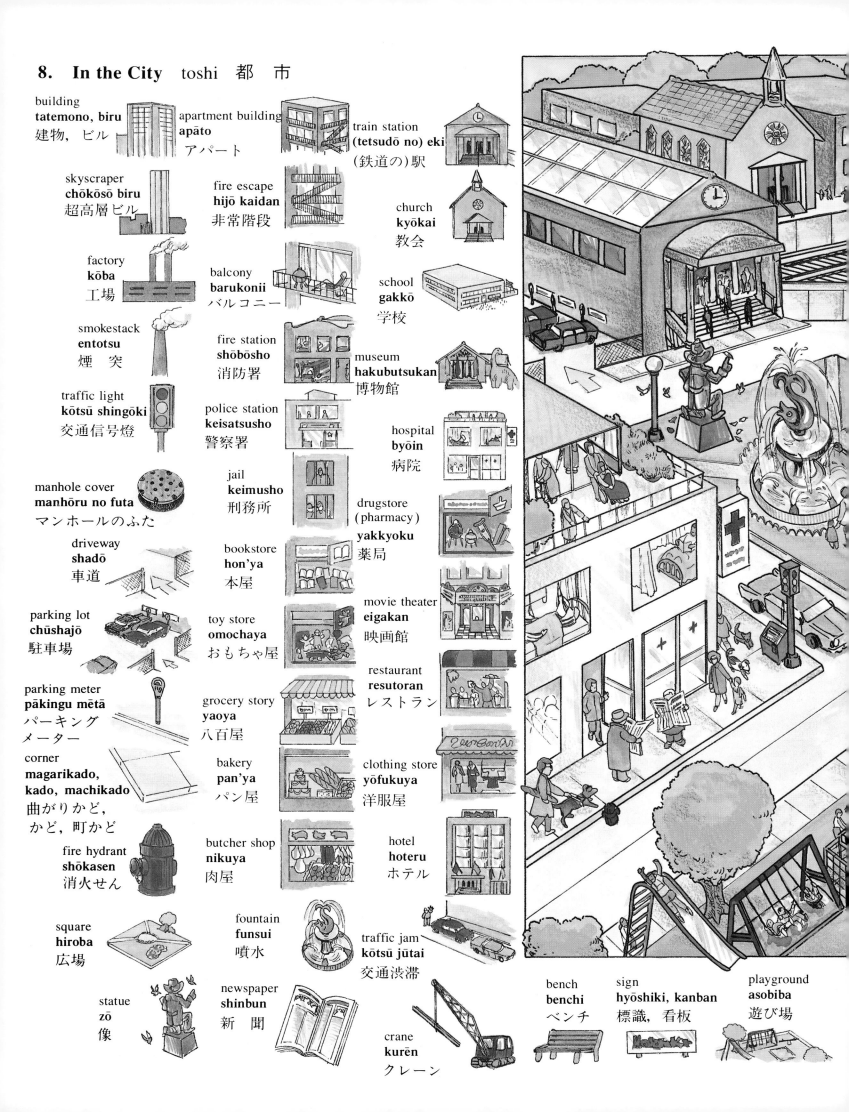

bench
benchi
ベンチ

sign
hyōshiki, kanban
標識，看板

playground
asobiba
遊び場

park	jungle gym	swings	seesaw	slide	sandbox	beach
kōen	**janguru jimu**	**buranko**	**shiisō**	**suberidai**	**sunaba**	**hama**
公園	ジャングルジム	ぶらんこ	シーソー	すべり台	砂場	浜

9. In the Country inaka 田舎

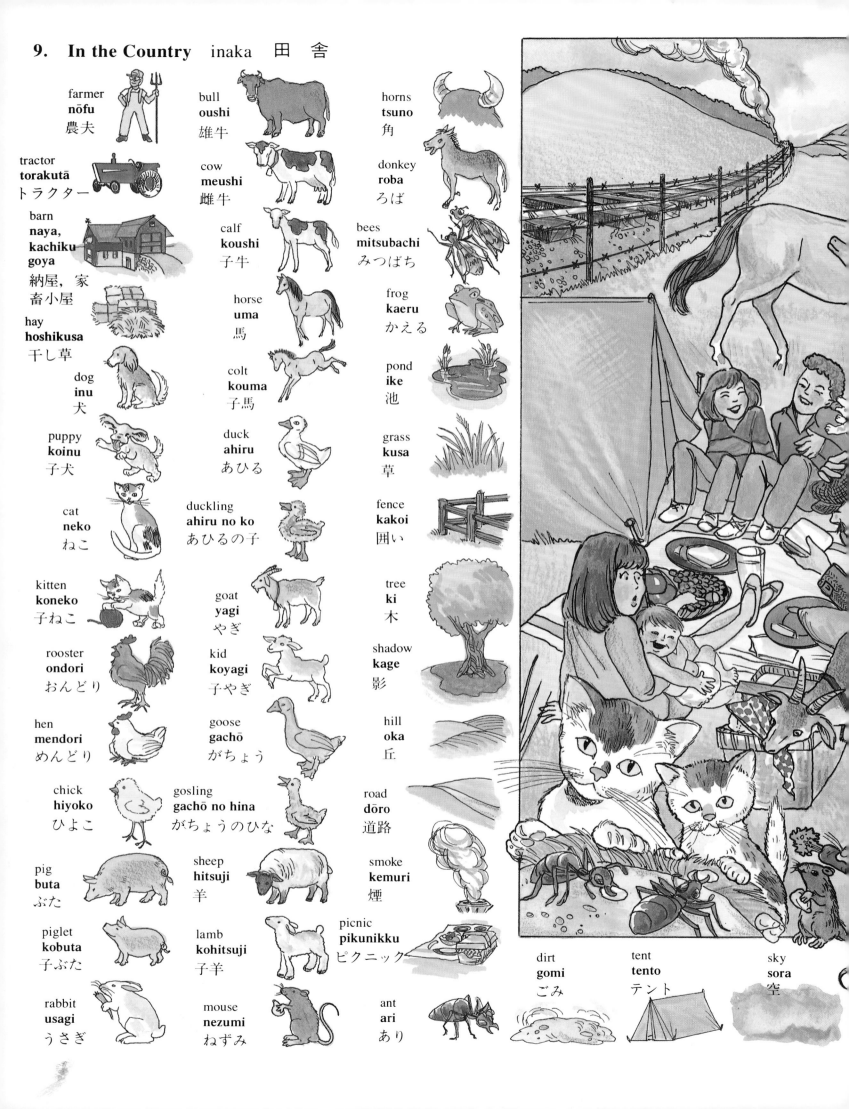

farmer
nōfu
農夫

tractor
torakutā
トラクター

barn
**naya,
kachiku
goya**
納屋，家
畜小屋

hay
hoshikusa
干し草

dog
inu
犬

puppy
koinu
子犬

cat
neko
ねこ

kitten
koneko
子ねこ

rooster
ondori
おんどり

hen
mendori
めんどり

chick
hiyoko
ひよこ

pig
buta
ぶた

piglet
kobuta
子ぶた

rabbit
usagi
うさぎ

bull
oushi
雄牛

cow
meushi
雌牛

calf
koushi
子牛

horse
uma
馬

colt
kouma
子馬

duck
ahiru
あひる

duckling
ahiru no ko
あひるの子

goat
yagi
やぎ

kid
koyagi
子やぎ

goose
gachō
がちょう

gosling
gachō no hina
がちょうのひな

sheep
hitsuji
羊

lamb
kohitsuji
子羊

mouse
nezumi
ねずみ

horns
tsuno
角

donkey
roba
ろば

bees
mitsubachi
みつばち

frog
kaeru
かえる

pond
ike
池

grass
kusa
草

fence
kakoi
囲い

tree
ki
木

shadow
kage
影

hill
oka
丘

road
dōro
道路

smoke
kemuri
煙

picnic
pikunikku
ピクニック

ant
ari
あり

dirt
gomi
ごみ

tent
tento
テント

sky
sora
空

train tracks
senro
線路

sleeping bag
nebukuro
寝袋

man
otoko
男

woman
onna
女

boy
shōnen
少年

girl
shōjo
少女

baby
akanbō
赤ん坊

farm
nōjō
農場

10. In a Restaurant resutoran レストラン

breakfast
chōshoku
朝食

lunch
**ranchi,
chūshoku**
ランチ,
昼食

dinner
yūshoku, dinā
夕食,
ディナー

yolk
kimi
黄身

hamburger
hanbāgā
ハンバーガー

steak
sutēki
ステーキ

omelet
omuretsu
オムレツ

sandwich
sandoitchi
サンドイッチ

fish
sakana
魚

toast
tōsuto
トースト

french fries
furenchi poteto
フレンチ
ポテト

ham
hamu
ハム

jam
jamu
ジャム

soup
sūpu
スープ

chicken
chikin, toriniku
チキン,
鶏肉

sausages
sōsēji
ソーセージ

noodles
menrui
めん類

broccoli
burokkorii
ブロッコリ

coffee
kōhii
コーヒー

ketchup
kechappu
ケチャップ

celery
serori
セロリ

tea
kōcha
紅茶

mustard
karashi, masutādo
からし,
マスタード

salad
sarada
サラダ

cream
kuriimu
クリーム

salt
shio
塩

rice
gohan
ごはん

sugar
satō
砂糖

pepper
koshō
こしょう

mushroom
masshurūmu
マッシュルーム

meals
shokuji
食事

ice cream
aisu kuriimu
アイスク
リーム

tray
bon, torē
盆, トレー

waiter
bōi, kyūji
ボーイ,
給仕

candle
rōsoku
ろうそく

tablecloth
tēburukurosu
テーブルクロス

waitress
uētoresu
ウエートレス

cake
kēki
ケーキ

straw
sutorō
ストロー

gift
okurimono
贈り物

birthday party
tanjō pātii
誕生パーティー

soft drink
sofuto dorinku, seiryō inryō (sui)
ソフトドリンク, 清涼飲料(水)

knife
naifu
ナイフ

fork
fōku
フォーク

spoon
supūn
スプーン

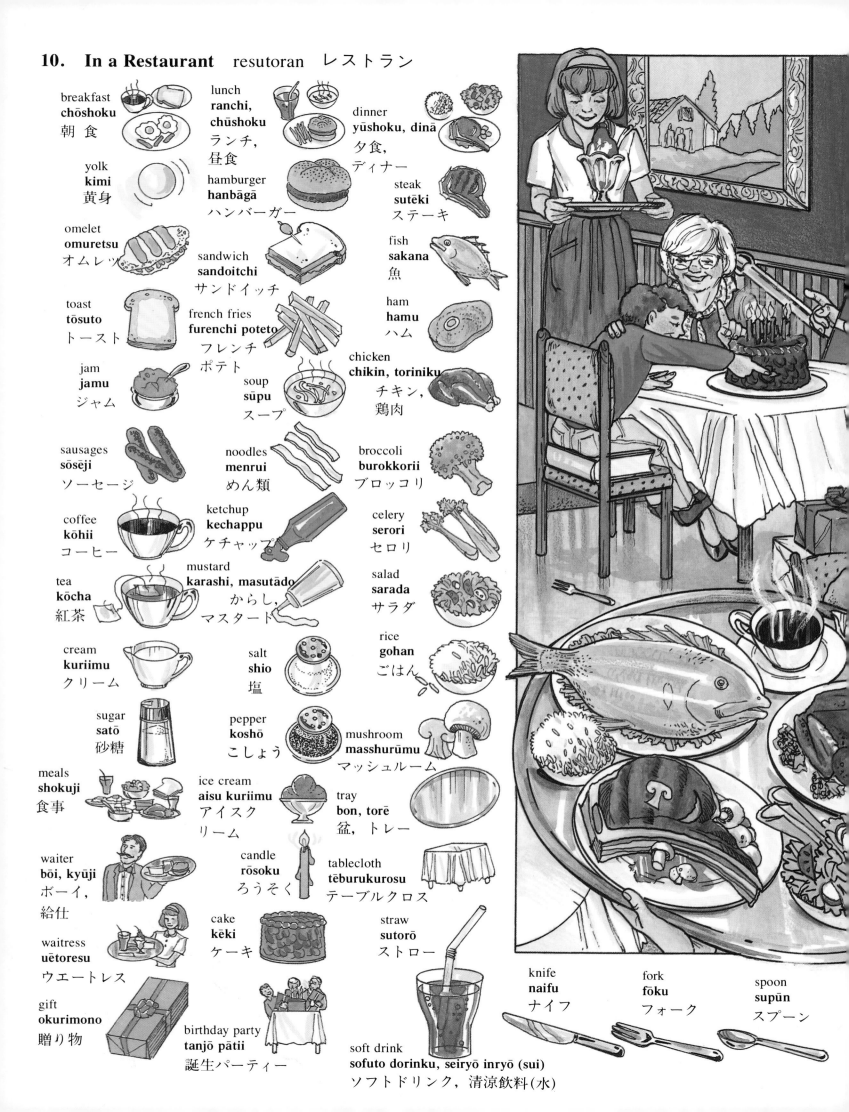

plate	saucer	cup	glass		napkin	menu
sara	**ukezare**	**kappu, chawan**	**koppu, gurasu**		**napukin**	**menyū**
皿	受け皿	カップ，茶わん	コップ，グラス		ナプキン	メニュー

bowl
bōru, donburi ボール，どんぶり

11. The Doctor's Office　iin　医　院

doctor
isha
医者

nurse
kangofu
看護婦

patient
kanja
患者

medicine
naifukuyaku
内服薬

pill
jōzai
錠剤

thermometer
taionkei
温度計

bandage
hōtai
包帯

cast
gipusu
ギプス

sling
tsuri hōtai
つり包帯

hypodermic needle
chūsha bari
注射針

blood
chi
血

cane
tsue
つえ

crutch
matsubazue
松葉づえ

stethoscope
chōshinki
聴診器

examining table
shinsatsudai
診察台

sneeze
kushami
くしゃみ

arm
ude
腕

elbow
hiji
ひじ

hand
te
手

finger
yubi
指

thumb
oyayubi
親指

leg
ashi
足

wheelchair
kuruma isu
車いす

foot
ashi
足

ankle
ashikubi
足首

toe
ashi no yubi
足の指

shoulder
kata
肩

back
se
背

chest
mune
胸

knee
hiza
ひざ

The Dentist's Office　shikaiin　歯科医院

dentist
haisha
歯医者

waiting room
machiaishitsu
待合室

dental hygienist
shika eisei gishi
歯科衛生技師

magazines
zasshi
雑誌

tooth
ha
歯

x ray
rentogen shashin
レントゲン写真

toothbrush
haburashi
歯ブラシ

smile
hohoemi
ほほえみ

toothpaste
nerihamigaki
ねり歯みがき

lips
kuchibiru
くちびる

dental floss
itoyōji
糸ようじ

tongue
shita
舌

eyebrow
mayu
まゆ

eyes
me
目

nose
hana
鼻

mouth
kuchi
口

chin
ago
あご

ear
mimi
耳

braces
shiretsu kyōseigu
歯列矯正具

head
atama
頭

face
kao
顔

cheek
hoho
ほほ

forehead
hitai
額

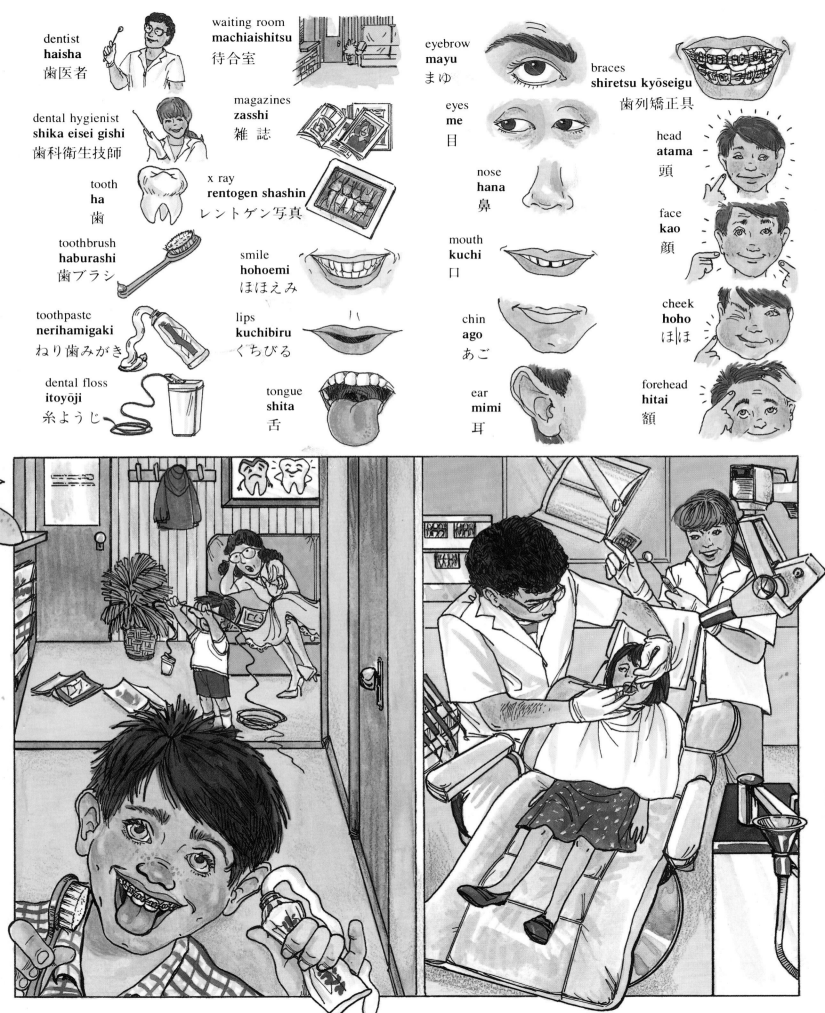

hairstylist
hea dezainā
ヘアデザイナー

mousse
(hea) mūsu
（ヘア）ムース

barrette
hea pin
ヘアピン

shampoo
shanpū
シャンプー

manicurist
manikyuashi
マニキュア師

braid
osagegame
おさげ髪

suds
sekken no awa
せっけんの
あわ

fingernail
yubi no tsume
指のつめ

wavy
uēbu no kakatta
ウエーブの
かかった

comb
kushi
くし

nail polish
nēru enameru
ネールエナメル

straight
**(chijirete inai)
massugu na**
（縮れていない）
まっすぐな

brush
burashi
ブラシ

lipstick
kuchibeni
口紅

curly
kāru shita
カールした

scissors
hasami
はさみ

mascara
masukara
マスカラ

short
mijikai
短い

curlers
kārā
カーラー

powder
oshiroi
おしろい

long
nagai
長い

curling iron
hea airon
ヘアアイロン

hair dryer
hea doraiyā
ヘアドライヤー

black
kuroi
黒い

barber
rihatsushi
理髪師

bald
hageta
はげた

brown
chairo no
茶色の

shaving cream
**higesoriyō
kuriimu**
ひげそり用
クリーム

mustache
kuchihige
口ひげ

blond
burondo no
ブロンドの

razor
kamisori
かみそり

freckles
sobakasu
そばかす

red
akai
赤い

toenail
ashiyubi no tsume
足指のつめ

beard
agohige
あごひげ

pedicurist
pedikyuashi
ペディキュア師

nail clippers
tsumekiri
つめ切り

nail file
tsumeyasuri
つめやすり

crew cut
kakugari
角刈り

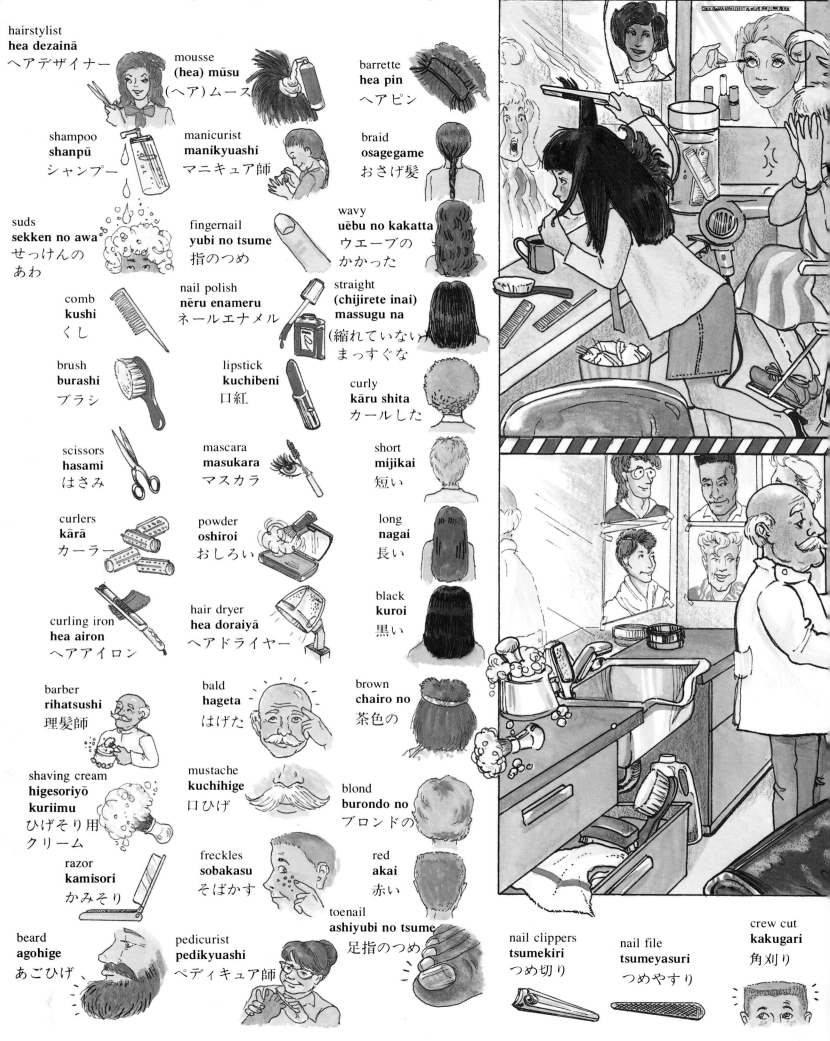

ponytail
poniitēru
ポニーテール

bangs
kirisage maegami
切り下げ前髪

bun
uzumakijō no sokuhatsu
うずまき状の
束髪

part
(tōhatsu no) wakeme
（頭髪の）
分け目

hair spray
hea supurē
ヘアスプレー

hair
tōhatsu
頭髪

blow dryer
hea doraiyā
ヘアドライヤー

13. The Post Office yūbinkyoku 郵便局

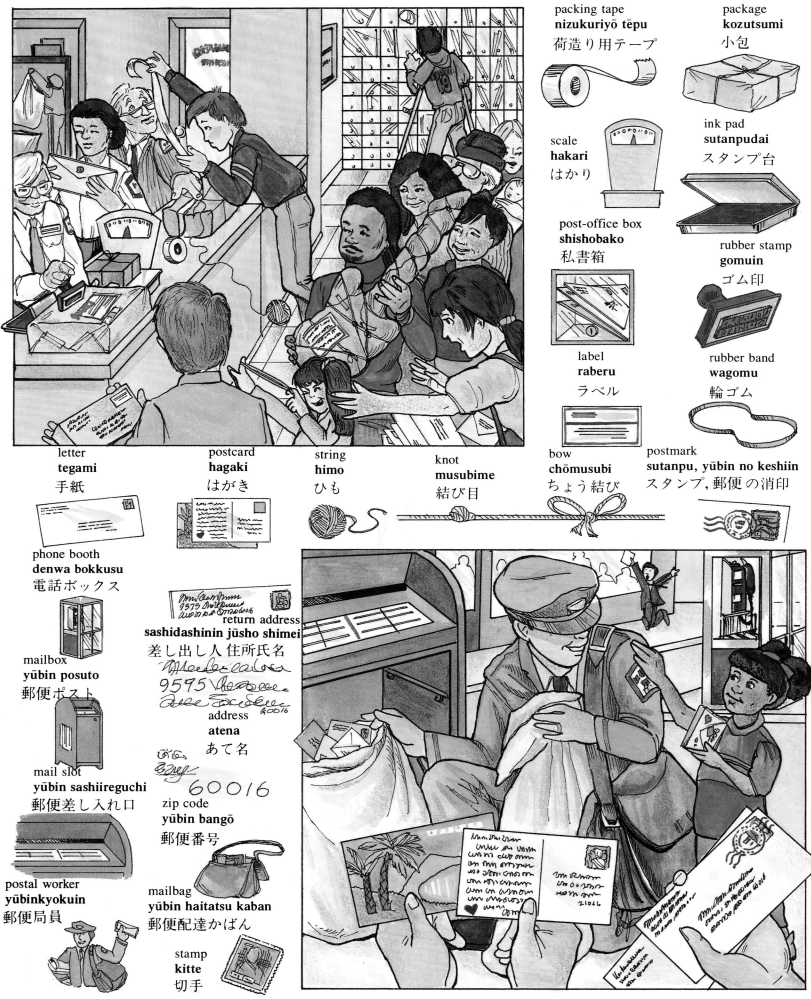

packing tape
nizukuriyō tēpu
荷造り用テープ

package
kozutsumi
小包

scale
hakari
はかり

ink pad
sutanpudai
スタンプ台

post-office box
shishobako
私書箱

rubber stamp
gomuin
ゴム印

label
raberu
ラベル

rubber band
wagomu
輪ゴム

letter
tegami
手紙

postcard
hagaki
はがき

string
himo
ひも

knot
musubime
結び目

bow
chōmusubi
ちょう結び

postmark
sutanpu, yūbin no keshiin
スタンプ, 郵便 の 消印

phone booth
denwa bokkusu
電話ボックス

mailbox
yūbin posuto
郵便ポスト

mail slot
yūbin sashiireguchi
郵便差し入れ口

postal worker
yūbinkyokuin
郵便局員

return address
sashidashinin jūsho shimei
差し出し人 住所氏名

address
atena
あて名

zip code
yūbin bangō
郵便番号

mailbag
yūbin haitatsu kaban
郵便配達かばん

stamp
kitte
切手

The Bank ginkō 銀行

paper clip
shorui tome kurippu
書類留めクリップ

security guard
keibiin
警備員

security camera
bōhan kamera
防犯カメラ

safe
kinko
金庫

credit card
kurejitto kādo
クレジットカード

typewriter
taipuraitā
タイプライター

safety deposit box
kashi kinko
貸金庫

notepad
memochō
メモ帳

file cabinet
shorui dana
書類棚

teller
kinsen suitō gakari
金銭出納係

wallet
saifu
さいふ

key
kagi
かぎ

lock
jō
錠

receptionist
uketsuke gakari
受付係

bill
shihei
紙幣

coin
kōka
硬貨

check
kogitte
小切手

checkbook
kogittechō
小切手帳

piggy bank
(buta no) chokinbako
（ぶたの）貯金箱

signature
sain
サイン

drive-in
doraibuin ginkō
ドライブイン銀行

automatic teller
jidō yokin shiharaiki
自動預金支払機

14. At the Gas Station   gasorin sutando ガソリンスタンド

mechanic
shūrikō
修理工

coveralls
tsunagi, kabarōru
つなぎ, カバロール

gas pump
gasorin ponpu
ガソリンポンプ

pliers
penchi
ペンチ

race car
kyōsōyō no kuruma
競走用の車

oil
sekiyu
石油

sunroof
sanrūfu
サンルーフ

dashboard
dasshubōdo
ダッシュボード

rag
borokire
ぼろきれ

garage
garēji
ガレージ

backseat
kōbu no zaseki
後部の座席

tow truck
rekkāsha
レッカー車

car wash
senshajō
洗車場

driver's seat
untenseki
運転席

truck driver
torakku no untenshu
トラックの運転手

gas cap
gasorin no futa
ガソリンのふた

passenger's seat
kyakuseki
客席

tank truck
tankusha
タンク車

tricycle
sanrinsha
三輪車

seat belt
shiito beruto
シートベルト

bicycle
jitensha
自転車

handlebars
handoru
ハンドル

hood
bonnetto
ボンネット

hand brake
hando burēki
ハンドブレーキ

reflectors
hanshakyō
反射鏡

engine
enjin
エンジン

bicycle chain
chēn
チェーン

pedal
pedaru
ペダル

trunk
toranku
トランク

spokes
supōku, (sharin no) ya
スポーク, (車輪の) 輻

kickstand
ippon sutando
一本スタンド

fender
fendā, doroyoke
フェンダー, どろよけ

training wheels
hojorin
補助輪

jack
jakki
ジャッキ

flat tire
panku shita taiya
パンクしたタイヤ

tire
taiya
タイヤ

hubcap
hoiiru kyappu
ホイールキャップ

headlight
heddoraito
ヘッドライト

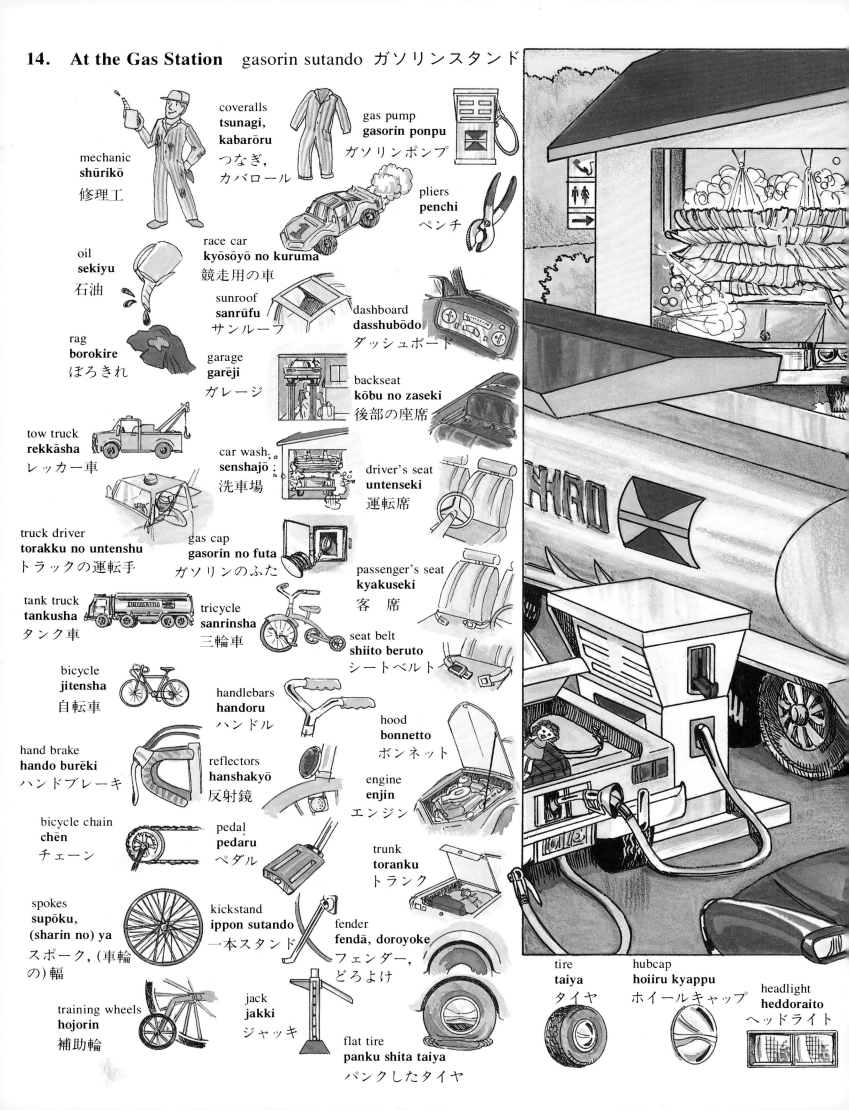

brake lights	windshield	windshield wipers	steering wheel	rearview mirror	air hose	door handle
burēki raito	**furonto garasu**	**waipā**	**handoru**	**bakku mirā**	**ea hōsu**	**doa no totte**
ブレーキライト	フロントガラス	ワイパー	ハンドル	バックミラー	エアホース	ドアの取っ手

15. People in Our Community chiiki no hitobito 地域の人々

saleswoman
onna ten'in, joshi ten'in
女店員

judge
saibankan
裁判官

cook
kokku
コック

model
moderu
モデル

electrician
denkikō
電気工

fire fighter
shōbōshi
消防士

athlete
supōtsuman
スポーツマン

doorman
doaman
ドアマン

architect
kenchikuka
建築家

plumber
kaikankō
配管工

bus driver
basu untenshu
バス運転手

television repairer
terebi shūrikō
テレビ修理工

taxi driver
takushii untenshu
タクシー運転手

fashion designer
fasshon dezainā
ファッション
デザイナー

tour guide
tsuā gaido
ツアーガイド

bookseller
hon'yasan
本屋さん

librarian
shisho
司 書

computer programmer
konpyūtā no puroguramā
コンピューターの
プログラマー

gardener
uekiya
植木屋

photographer
kameraman
カメラマン

painter
penkiya
ペンキ屋

salesman
danshi ten'in
男子店員

secretary
hisho
秘書

weather forecaster
tenki yohō gakari
天気予報係

veterinarian
jūi
獣医

policewoman
fujin keikan
婦人警官

disc jockey
disuku jokkii
ディスクジョッキー

reporter
repōtā
レポーター

tailor
yōfukuya
洋服屋

construction worker
kensetsu sagyōin
建設作業員

florist
hanaya
花屋

factory worker
kōin
工 員

butcher
nikuyasan
肉屋さん

jeweler
hōsekishō
宝石商

foreman
genba kantoku
現場監督

optician
meganeya
めがね屋

carpenter
daiku
大工

banker
ginkōka
銀行家

artist
gaka
画家

pharmacist
kusuriya
薬屋

sailor
suihei
水兵

lawyer
bengoshi
弁護士

paramedic
kyūkyū taiin
救急隊員

letter carrier
yūbin shūhainin
郵便集配人

fisherman
ryōshi
漁師

cowboy
kaubōi
カウボーイ

policeman
keikan
警官

astronomer
tenmon gakusha
天文学者

16. Going Places (Transportation) yusō kikan 輸送機関

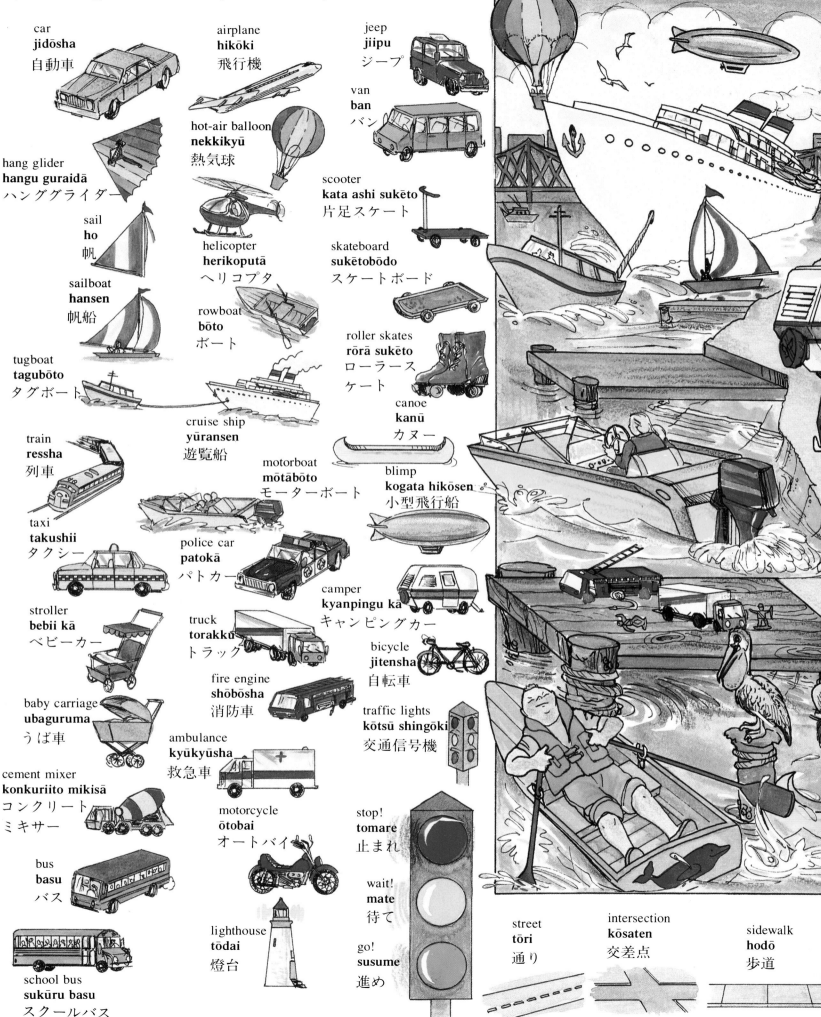

car
jidōsha
自動車

hang glider
hangu guraidā
ハンググライダー

sail
ho
帆

sailboat
hansen
帆船

tugboat
tagubōto
タグボート

train **ressha**
列車

taxi
takushii
タクシー

stroller
bebii kā
ベビーカー

baby carriage
ubaguruma
うば車

cement mixer
konkuriito mikisā
コンクリート
ミキサー

bus
basu
バス

school bus
sukūru basu
スクールバス

airplane
hikōki
飛行機

hot-air balloon
nekkikyū
熱気球

helicopter
herikoputā
ヘリコプタ

rowboat
bōto
ボート

cruise ship
yūransen
遊覧船

motorboat
mōtābōto
モーターボート

police car
patokā
パトカー

truck
torakku
トラック

fire engine
shōbōsha
消防車

ambulance
kyūkyūsha
救急車

motorcycle
ōtobai
オートバイ

lighthouse
tōdai
燈台

jeep
jiipu
ジープ

van
ban
バン

scooter
kata ashi sukēto
片足スケート

skateboard
sukētobōdo
スケートボード

roller skates
rōrā sukēto
ローラース
ケート

canoe
kanū
カヌー

blimp
kogata hikōsen
小型飛行船

camper
kyanpingu kā
キャンピングカー

bicycle
jitensha
自転車

traffic lights
kōtsū shingōki
交通信号機

stop!
tomare
止まれ

wait!
mate
待て

go!
susume
進め

street
tōri
通り

intersection
kōsaten
交差点

sidewalk
hodō
歩道

dock
funatsukiba
船着き場

bus stop
basu no teiryūjo
バスの停留所

bridge
hashi
橋

crosswalk
ōdan hodō
横断歩道

oar
ōru
オール

boat
bōto
ボート

stop sign
teishi no hyōshiki
停止の標識

17. The Airport kūkō 空港

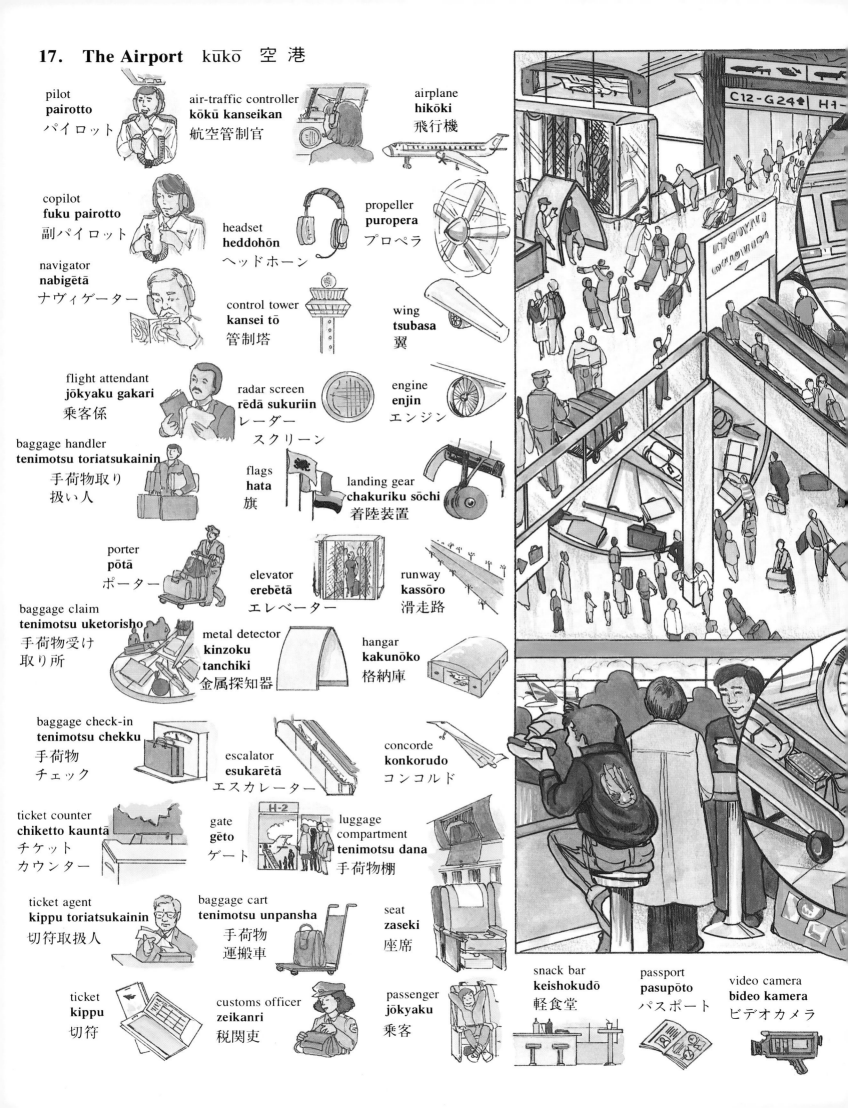

pilot
pairotto
パイロット

air-traffic controller
kōkū kanseikan
航空管制官

airplane
hikōki
飛行機

copilot
fuku pairotto
副パイロット

headset
heddohōn
ヘッドホーン

propeller
puropera
プロペラ

navigator
nabigētā
ナヴィゲーター

control tower
kansei tō
管制塔

wing
tsubasa
翼

flight attendant
jōkyaku gakari
乗客係

radar screen
rēdā sukuriin
レーダー
スクリーン

engine
enjin
エンジン

baggage handler
tenimotsu toriatsukainin
手荷物取り
扱い人

flags
hata
旗

landing gear
chakuriku sōchi
着陸装置

porter
pōtā
ポーター

elevator
erebētā
エレベーター

runway
kassōro
滑走路

baggage claim
tenimotsu uketorisho
手荷物受け
取り所

metal detector
kinzoku tanchiki
金属探知器

hangar
kakunōko
格納庫

baggage check-in
tenimotsu chekku
手荷物
チェック

escalator
esukarētā
エスカレーター

concorde
konkorudo
コンコルド

ticket counter
chiketto kauntā
チケット
カウンター

gate
gēto
ゲート

luggage
compartment
tenimotsu dana
手荷物棚

ticket agent
kippu toriatsukainin
切符取扱人

baggage cart
tenimotsu unpansha
手荷物
運搬車

seat
zaseki
座席

ticket
kippu
切符

customs officer
zeikanri
税関吏

passenger
jōkyaku
乗客

snack bar
keishokudō
軽食堂

passport
pasupōto
パスポート

video camera
bideo kamera
ビデオカメラ

binoculars
sōgankyō
双眼鏡

camera
kamera
カメラ

purse
handobaggu
ハンドバッグ

suitcase
sūtsukēsu
スーツケース

garment bag
ishōire kaban
衣装入れかばん

briefcase
shorui kaban
書類かばん

tennis racket
tenisu no raketto
テニスのラケット

18. Sports supōtsu スポーツ

gymnastics
taisō
体操

goggles
gōguru
ゴーグル

wrestling **resuringu**
レスリング

cross-country skiing
kurosu-kantorii sukii
クロスカントリースキー

cycling
jitensha kyōsō 自転車競走

soccer
sakkā
サッカー

long jump
habatobi
幅飛び

car racing
kā rēsu
カーレース

baseball
(yakyūyō) bōru
(野球用)ボール

boxing
bokushingu
ボクシング

badminton
badominton
バドミントン

net
netto
ネット

football
amerikan futtobōru
アメリカンフットボール

skates
sukēto gutsu
スケート靴

skating
sukēto
スケート

hurdles
shōgai kyōsō
障害競走

golf
gorufu
ゴルフ

medal
medaru
メダル

horseback riding
jōba
乗　馬

baseball
yakyū
野球

jogging
jogingu
ジョギング

hockey
aisu hokkē
アイスホッケー

tennis
tenisu
テニス

diving
tobikomi
飛び込み

weight lifting
jūryōage
重量あげ

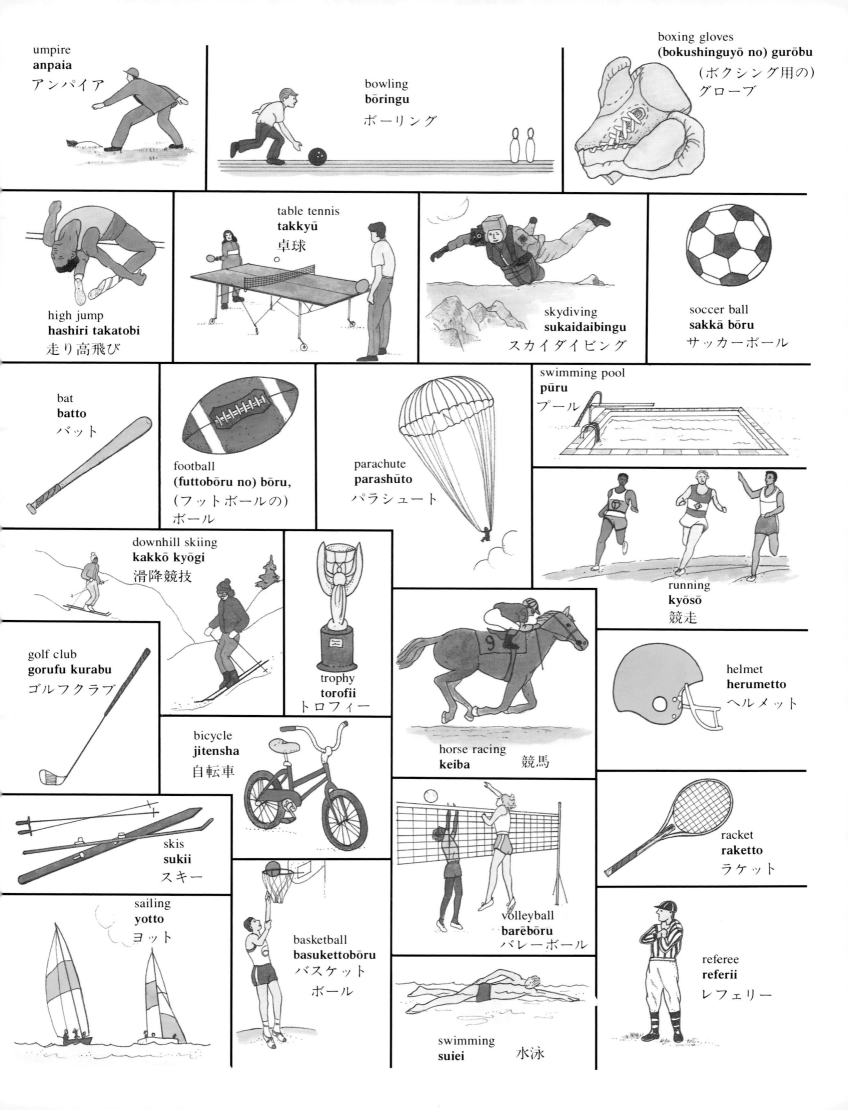

umpire
anpaia
アンパイア

bowling
bōringu
ボーリング

boxing gloves
(bokushinguyō no) gurōbu
（ボクシング用の）
グローブ

high jump
hashiri takatobi
走り高飛び

table tennis
takkyū
卓球

skydiving
sukaidaibingu
スカイダイビング

soccer ball
sakkā bōru
サッカーボール

bat
batto
バット

football
(futtobōru no) bōru,
（フットボールの）
ボール

parachute
parashūto
パラシュート

swimming pool
pūru
プール

running
kyōsō
競走

downhill skiing
kakkō kyōgi
滑降競技

golf club
gorufu kurabu
ゴルフクラブ

trophy
torofii
トロフィー

horse racing
keiba　競馬

helmet
herumetto
ヘルメット

bicycle
jitensha
自転車

racket
raketto
ラケット

skis
sukii
スキー

sailing
yotto
ヨット

basketball
basukettobōru
バスケット
ボール

volleyball
barēbōru
バレーボール

swimming
suiei　水泳

referee
referii
レフェリー

19. The Talent Show   tarento shō   タレントショー

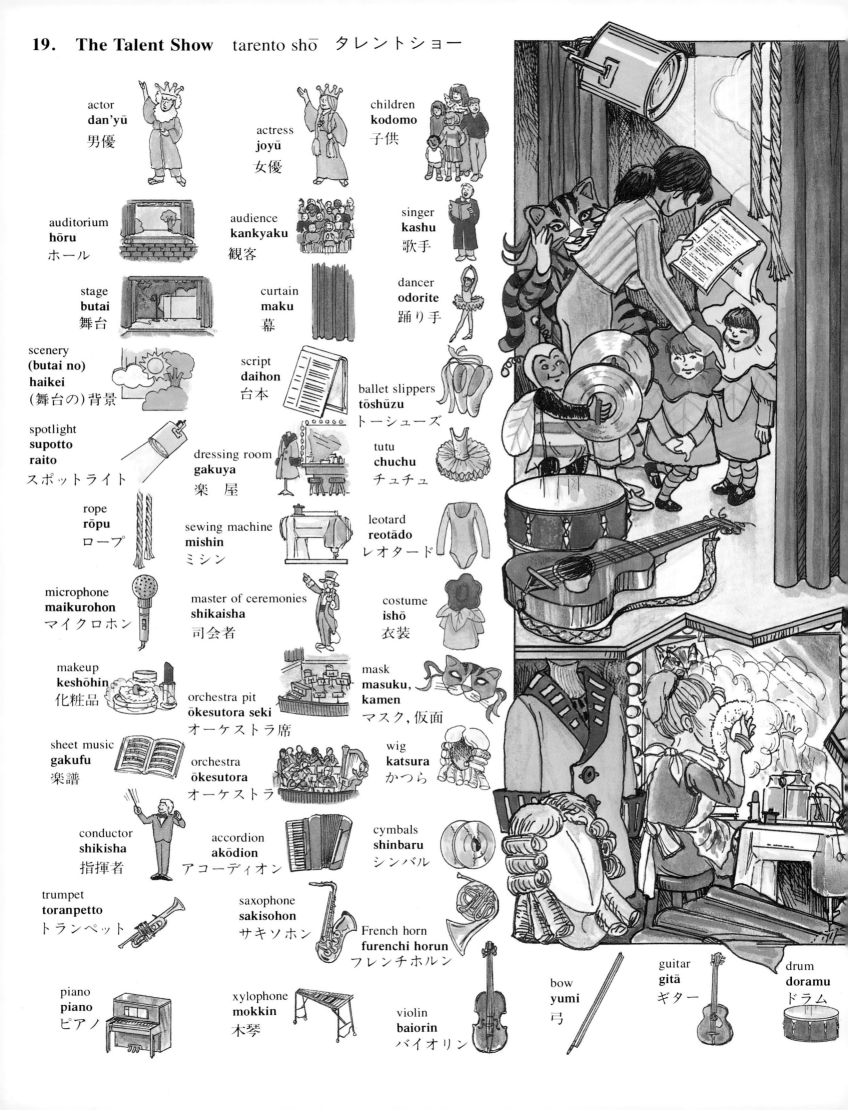

actor
dan'yū
男優

actress
joyū
女優

children
kodomo
子供

auditorium
hōru
ホール

audience
kankyaku
観客

singer
kashu
歌手

stage
butai
舞台

curtain
maku
幕

dancer
odorite
踊り手

scenery
**(butai no)
haikei**
(舞台の)背景

script
daihon
台本

ballet slippers
tōshūzu
トーシューズ

spotlight
**supotto
raito**
スポットライト

dressing room
gakuya
楽屋

tutu
chuchu
チュチュ

rope
rōpu
ロープ

sewing machine
mishin
ミシン

leotard
reotādo
レオタード

microphone
maikurohon
マイクロホン

master of ceremonies
shikaisha
司会者

costume
ishō
衣装

makeup
keshōhin
化粧品

orchestra pit
ōkesutora seki
オーケストラ席

mask
**masuku,
kamen**
マスク, 仮面

sheet music
gakufu
楽譜

orchestra
ōkesutora
オーケストラ

wig
katsura
かつら

conductor
shikisha
指揮者

accordion
akōdion
アコーディオン

cymbals
shinbaru
シンバル

trumpet
toranpetto
トランペット

saxophone
sakisohon
サキソホン

French horn
furenchi horun
フレンチホルン

piano
piano
ピアノ

xylophone
mokkin
木琴

violin
baiorin
バイオリン

bow
yumi
弓

guitar
gitā
ギター

drum
doramu
ドラム

tuba **chūba** チューバ
flute **furūto** フルート
trombone **toronbōn** トロンボーン
clarinet **kurarinetto** クラリネット
cello **chero** チェロ
strings **gen** 弦
harp **hāpu** ハープ

20. At the Zoo dōbutsuen 動物園

zookeeper
shiiku gakari
飼育係

elephant
zō
象

animals
dōbutsu
動物

rhinoceros
sai
さい

ostrich
dachō
だちょう

fox
kitsune
きつね

lion
raion
ライオン

bear
kuma
くま

wolf
ōkami
おおかみ

tiger
tora
とら

bear cub
koguma
子ぐま

alligator
arigētā, wani
アリゲーター, わに

tiger cub
tora no ko
とらの子

polar bear
shirokuma
白くま

zebra
shimauma
しま馬

jaguar
jagā
ジャガー

panda
panda
パンダ

giraffe
kirin
きりん

leopard
hyō
ひょう

gorilla
gorira
ゴリラ

monkey
saru
さる

flamingo
furamingo
フラミンゴ

parrot
ōmu
おうむ

hippopotamus
kaba
かば

owl
fukurō
ふくろう

snake
hebi
へび

kangaroo
kangarū
カンガルー

swan
hakuchō
白鳥

seal
azarashi
あざらし

deer
shika
しか

penguin
pengin
ペンギン

walrus
seiuchi
せいうち

lizard
tokage
とかげ

peacock
(osu no) kujaku
(雄の)くじゃく

hump
(rakuda no) kobu
(らくだの)こぶ

turtle
umigame
海がめ

eagle
washi
わし

camel
rakuda
らくだ

horns
tsuno
角

wings
hane, tsubasa
羽, 翼

beak
kuchibashi
くちばし

feathers
umō
羽毛

paw
ashi
足

claws
tsume
つめ

mane
tategami
たてがみ

tail
o
尾

hoof
hizume
ひづめ

stripes
shima
しま

spots
hanten
はん点

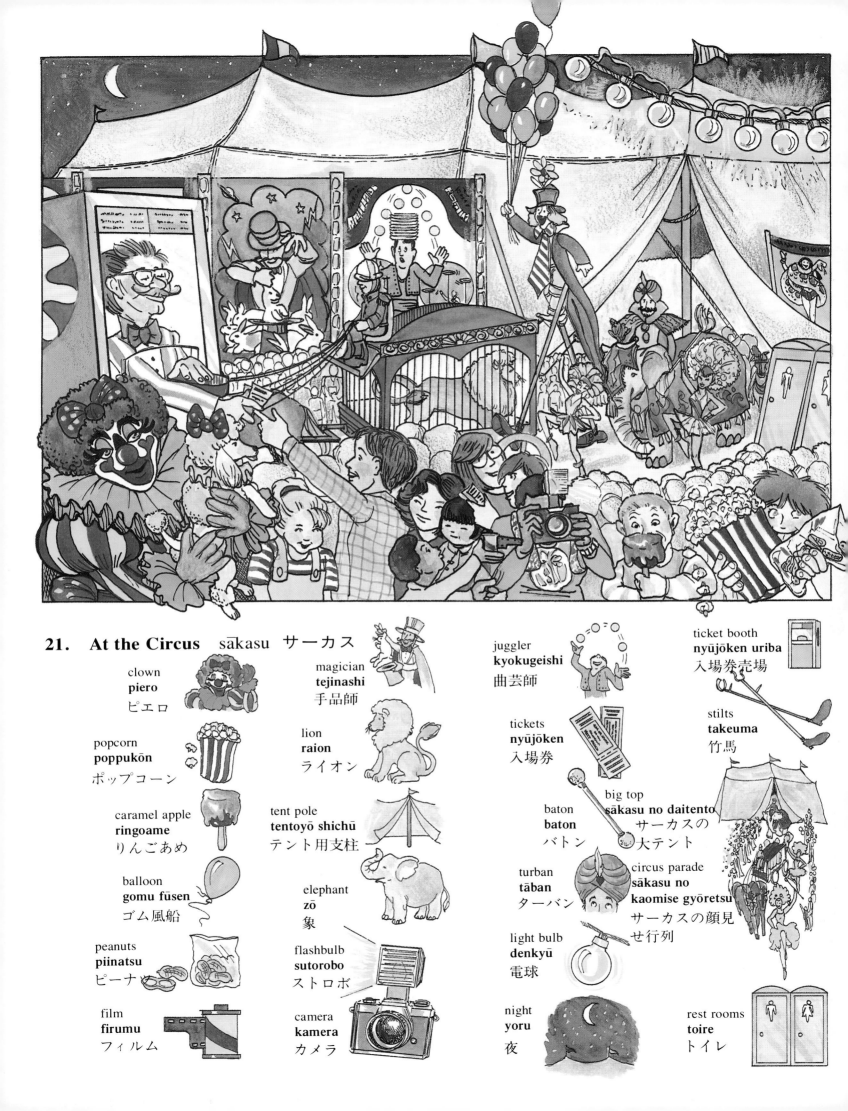

21. At the Circus　sākasu　サーカス

clown
piero
ピエロ

popcorn
poppukōn
ポップコーン

caramel apple
ringoame
りんごあめ

balloon
gomu fūsen
ゴム風船

peanuts
piinatsu
ピーナツ

film
firumu
フィルム

magician
tejinashi
手品師

lion
raion
ライオン

tent pole
tentoyō shichū
テント用支柱

elephant
zō
象

flashbulb
sutorobo
ストロボ

camera
kamera
カメラ

juggler
kyokugeishi
曲芸師

tickets
nyūjōken
入場券

baton
baton
バトン

turban
tāban
ターバン

light bulb
denkyū
電球

night
yoru
夜

ticket booth
nyūjōken uriba
入場券売場

stilts
takeuma
竹馬

big top
sākasu no daitento
サーカスの
大テント

circus parade
**sākasu no
kaomise gyōretsu**
サーカスの顔見
せ行列

rest rooms
toire
トイレ

bareback rider
kyokunori
曲乗り

tightrope walker
tsunawatari
綱渡り

trapeze
buranko
ぶらんこ

trapeze artist
burankonori
ぶらんこ乗り

tightrope
tsuna
綱

cage
ori
おり

band
gakudan
楽団

whip
muchi
むち

safety net
anzen netto
安全ネット

lion tamer
raion zukai
ライオン使い

unicycle
ichirinsha
一輪車

handstand
sakadachi
さか立ち

headstand
(ryōte to atama o shita ni tsukete suru) sakadachi
(両手と頭を
下につけて
する)さか立ち

acrobat
karuwazashi
軽わざ師

somersault
bakuten
ばくてん

ring
wa
輪

cartwheel
yoko tonbogaeri
横とんぼ返り

hoop
wa
輪

cotton candy
watagashi
綿菓子

rope ladder
nawabashigo
なわばしご

cape
katamanto
肩マント

rope
nawa
なわ

ringmaster
engi kantoku
演技監督

22. In the Ocean umi 海

scuba diver
sukyuba daibā
スキュバ
ダイバー

wet suit
uetto sūtsu
ウエット
スーツ

flipper
ashihire
足ひれ

oxygen tank
sanso bonbe
酸素ボンベ

snorkel
shunōkeru
シュノーケル

mask
masuku,
suichū megane
マスク，水中めがね

starfish
hitode
ひとで

jellyfish
kurage
くらげ

sea turtle
umigame
うみがめ

lobster
robusutā
ロブスター

stingray
akaei
あかえい

dolphin
iruka
いるか

shark
same, fuka
さめ,ふか

octopus
tako
たこ

tentacle
shokushu
触手

swordfish
mekajiki
めかじき

angelfish
enzerufisshu
エンゼルフィッシュ

school (of fish)
mure
群れ

fishing line
tsuri ito
つり糸

fishhook
tsuribari
つり針

buoy
bui
ブイ

submarine
sensuikan
潜水艦

porthole
gensō
舷窓

sea urchin
uni
うに

sea horse
tatsu no otoshigo
たつのおとしご

seaweed
kaisō
海草

shipwreck
nanpasen
難破船

helm
kaji
かじ

cannon
taihō
大砲

anchor
ikari
いかり

treasure chest
hōsekibako
宝石箱

treasure
zaihō
財宝

gold
kinka
金貨

silver
ginka
銀貨

jewel
hōseki
宝石

barnacle
fujitsubo
ふじつぼ

coral
sango
さんご

coral reef
sangoshō
さんご礁

seashell
kai
貝

wave
nami
波

sand
sunahama
砂浜

bubble
awa, kihō
あわ，気泡

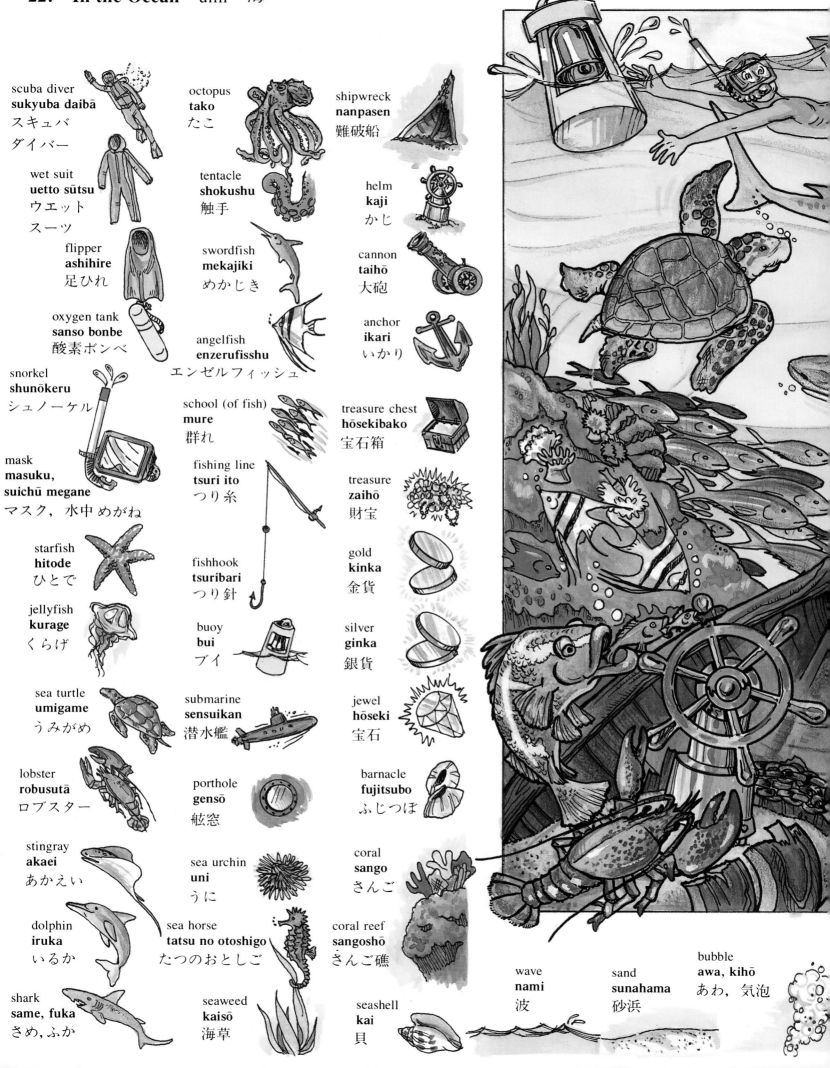

scales
uroko
うろこ

gills
era
えら

fin
hire
ひれ

clam
hamaguri
はまぐり

crab
kani
かに

squid
yariika
やりいか

whale
kujira
鯨

23. Space　uchū　宇宙

astronaut
uchū hikōshi
宇宙飛行士

space suit
uchū fuku
宇宙服

space helmet
uchū herumetto
宇宙ヘル
メット

footprint
ashiato
足跡

space walk
uchū yūei
宇宙遊泳

moon rock
tsuki no ishi
月の石

space shuttle
supēsu shatoru
スペースシャトル

lunar rover
getsumensha
月面車

laboratory
kenkyūshitsu
研究室

cargo bay
nimotsu shitsu
荷物室

landing capsule
chakuriku kapuseru
着陸カプ
セル

scientist
kagakusha
科学者

control panel
seigyo ban
制御盤

ladder
hashigo
はしご

lab coat
jikkengi
実験着

satellite
jinkō eisei
人工衛星

space station
uchū sutēshon
宇宙ステーション

microscope
kenbikyō
顕微鏡

computer
konpyūtā
コンピューター

spaceship
uchūsen
宇宙船

solar panel
taiyō denchiban
太陽電池板

alien
uchūjin
宇宙人

meteor shower
ryūseiu
流星雨

beaker
biikā
ビーカー

antenna
antena
アンテナ

test tube
shikenkan
試験管

constellation
seiza
星　座

galaxy
gingakei
銀河系

asteroid
shōwakusei
小惑星

solar system
taiyōkei
太陽系

earth
chikyū
地球

moon
tsuki
月

sun
taiyō
太陽

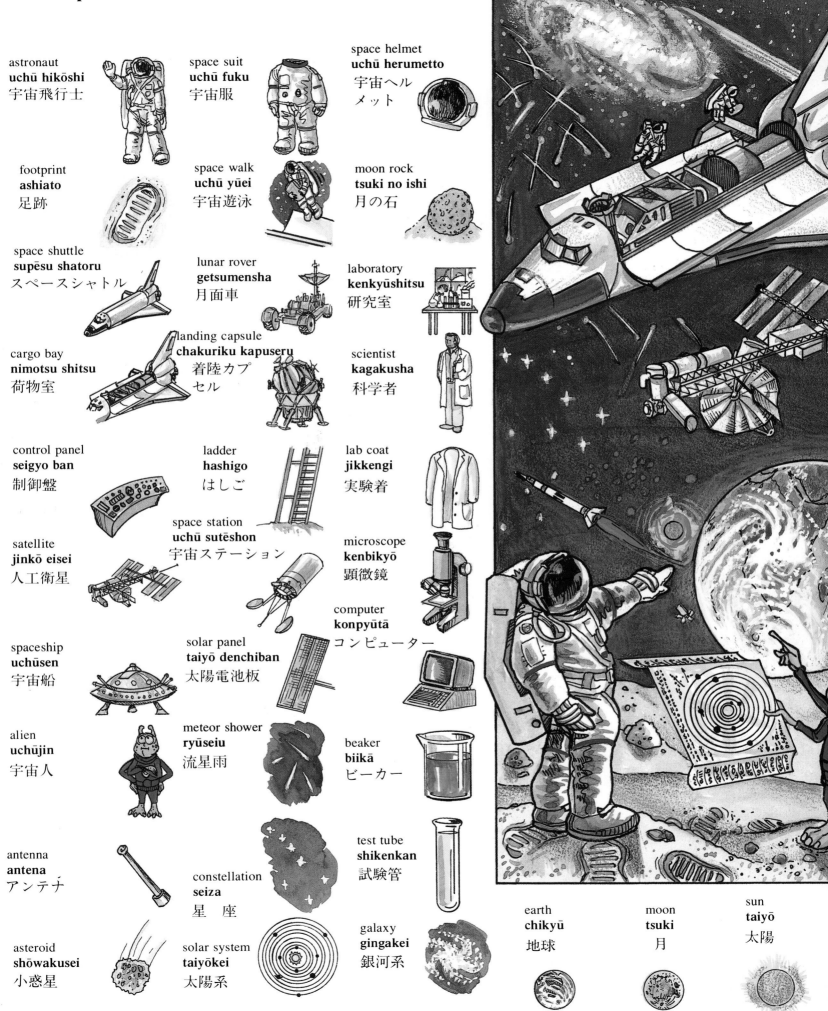

planet	rings	crater	stars	comet	nebula	rocket	robot
wakusei	**(wakusei no) wa**	**kurētā**	**hoshi**	**suisei**	**seiun**	**roketto**	**robotto**
惑星	（惑星の）輪	クレーター	星	すい星	星雲	ロケット	ロボット

24. Human History   jinrui no rekishi   人類の歴史

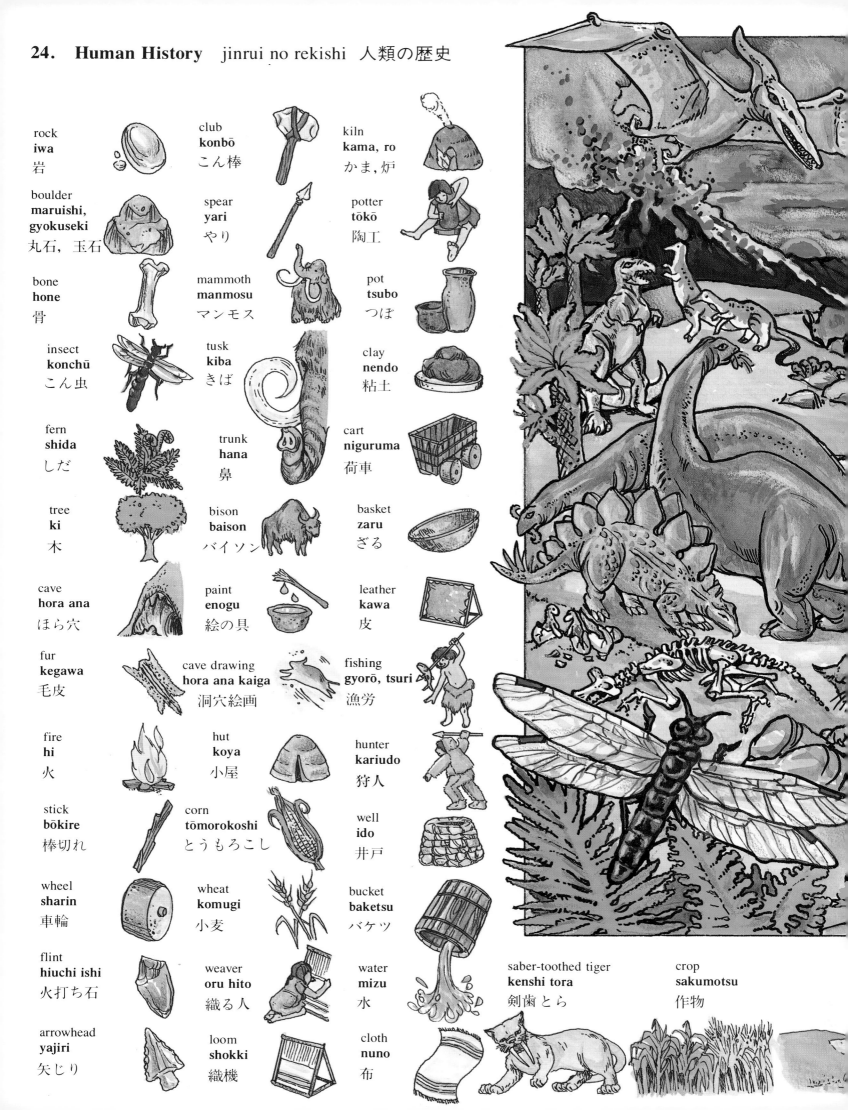

rock
iwa
岩

boulder
**maruishi,
gyokuseki**
丸石，玉石

bone
hone
骨

insect
konchū
こん虫

fern
shida
しだ

tree
ki
木

cave
hora ana
ほら穴

fur
kegawa
毛皮

fire
hi
火

stick
bōkire
棒切れ

wheel
sharin
車輪

flint
hiuchi ishi
火打ち石

arrowhead
yajiri
矢じり

club
konbō
こん棒

spear
yari
やり

mammoth
manmosu
マンモス

tusk
kiba
きば

trunk
hana
鼻

bison
baison
バイソン

paint
enogu
絵の具

cave drawing
hora ana kaiga
洞穴絵画

hut
koya
小屋

corn
tōmorokoshi
とうもろこし

wheat
komugi
小麦

weaver
oru hito
織る人

loom
shokki
織機

kiln
kama, ro
かま，炉

potter
tōkō
陶工

pot
tsubo
つぼ

clay
nendo
粘土

cart
niguruma
荷車

basket
zaru
ざる

leather
kawa
皮

fishing
gyorō, tsuri
漁労

hunter
kariudo
狩人

well
ido
井戸

bucket
baketsu
バケツ

water
mizu
水

cloth
nuno
布

saber-toothed tiger
kenshi tora
剣歯とら

crop
sakumotsu
作物

field
hatake
畑

village
sonraku
村落

cave dwellers
ana kyojin
穴居人

skeleton
kokkaku
骨格

dinosaur
kyōryū
恐竜

pterodactyl
yokuryū
翼竜

25. The Make-Believe Castle maboroshi no oshiro まぼろしのお城

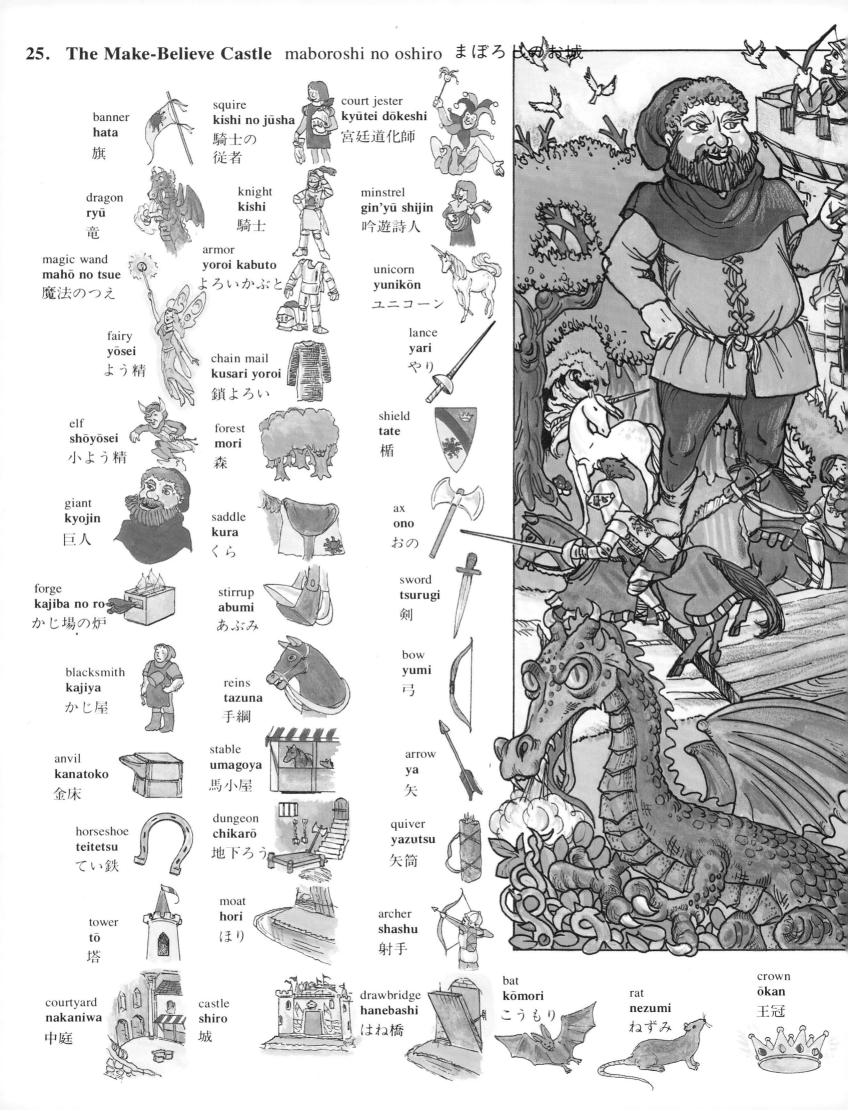

banner
hata
旗

squire
kishi no jūsha
騎士の
従者

court jester
kyūtei dōkeshi
宮廷道化師

dragon
ryū
竜

knight
kishi
騎士

minstrel
gin'yū shijin
吟遊詩人

magic wand
mahō no tsue
魔法のつえ

armor
yoroi kabuto
よろいかぶと

unicorn
yunikōn
ユニコーン

fairy
yōsei
よう精

chain mail
kusari yoroi
鎖よろい

lance
yari
やり

elf
shōyōsei
小よう精

forest
mori
森

shield
tate
楯

giant
kyojin
巨人

saddle
kura
くら

ax
ono
おの

forge
kajiba no ro
かじ場の炉

stirrup
abumi
あぶみ

sword
tsurugi
剣

blacksmith
kajiya
かじ屋

reins
tazuna
手綱

bow
yumi
弓

anvil
kanatoko
金床

stable
umagoya
馬小屋

arrow
ya
矢

horseshoe
teitetsu
てい鉄

dungeon
chikarō
地下ろう

quiver
yazutsu
矢筒

tower
tō
塔

moat
hori
ほり

archer
shashu
射手

courtyard
nakaniwa
中庭

castle
shiro
城

drawbridge
hanebashi
はね橋

bat
kōmori
こうもり

rat
nezumi
ねずみ

crown
ōkan
王冠

king
ō
王

queen
joō
女王

princess
ōjo
王女

prince
ōji
王子

throne
gyokuza
玉座

spider
kumo
くも

spiderweb
kumo no su
くもの巣

26. The Mouse Hunt (Prepositions and Adjectives)
nezumitori (zenchishi to keiyōshi) ねずみとり（前置詞と形容詞）

behind
. . . no ushiro ni
…のうしろに

good
yoi
よい

above
. . . no ue ni
…の上に

on top of
. . . no ue ni
…の上に

in front of
. . . no mae ni
…の前に

inside
uchigawa no
内側の

outside
sotogawa no
外側の

bad
warui
悪い

under
. . . no shita ni
…の下に

soft
yawarakai
柔らかい

next to
. . . ni mottomo chikai
…に最も近い

tall
sei no takai
背の高い

wide
haba no hiroi
幅の広い

narrow
haba ga semai
幅が狭い

short
sei ga hikui
背が低い

heavy
omoi
重い

difficult
muzukashii
むずかしい

large
ōkina
大きな

medium
chūgurai no
中位の

small
chiisai
小さい

dry
kawaita
かわいた

wet
nureta
ぬれた

full
ippai no　いっぱいの

empty
kara no　からの

fat
futotta
太った

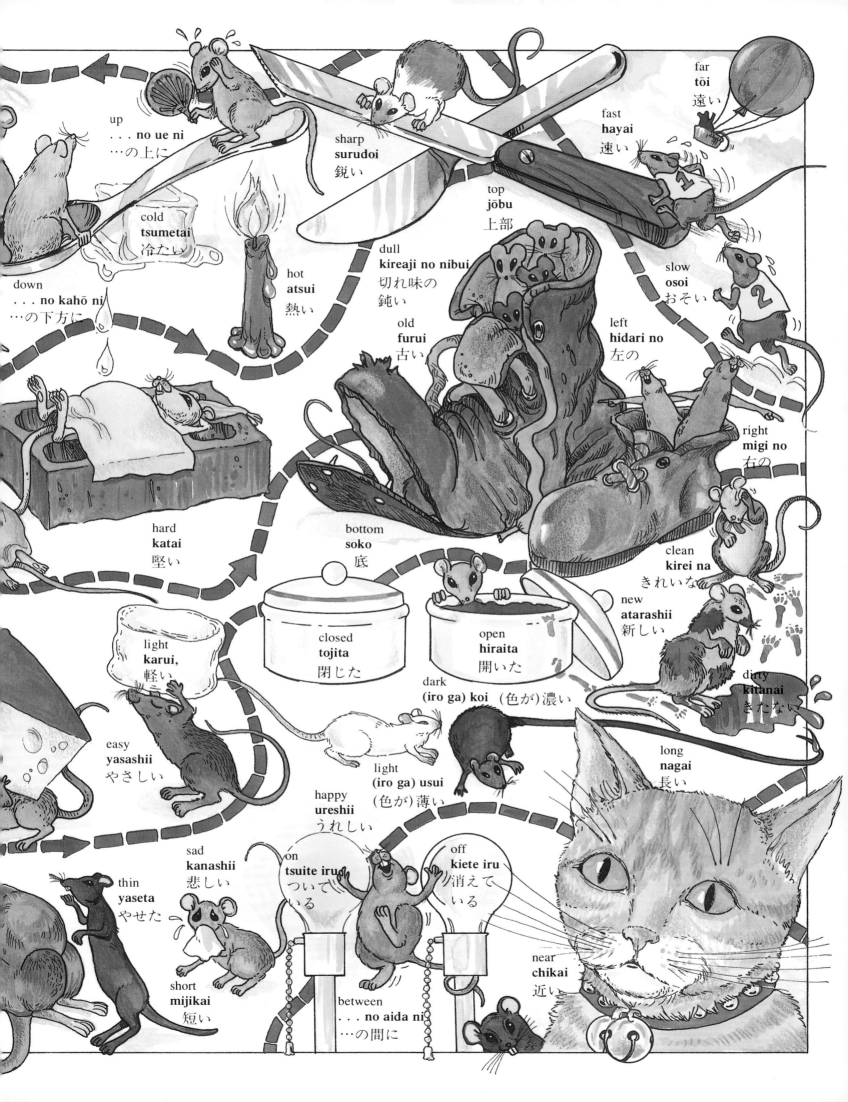

up
. . . no ue ni
…の上に

cold
tsumetai
冷たい

down
. . . no kahō ni
…の下方に

hot
atsui
熱い

sharp
surudoi
鋭い

dull
kireaji no nibui
切れ味の
鈍い

old
furui
古い

top
jōbu
上部

far
tōi
遠い

fast
hayai
速い

slow
osoi
おそい

left
hidari no
左の

right
migi no
右の

hard
katai
堅い

bottom
soko
底

clean
kirei na
きれいな

new
atarashii
新しい

light
karui,
軽い

closed
tojita
閉じた

open
hiraita
開いた

dirty
kitanai
きたない

easy
yasashii
やさしい

dark
(iro ga) koi （色が）濃い

light
(iro ga) usui
（色が）薄い

long
nagai
長い

happy
ureshii
うれしい

sad
kanashii
悲しい

on
tsuite iru
ついて
いる

off
kiete iru
消えて
いる

thin
yaseta
やせた

short
mijikai
短い

between
. . . no aida ni
…の間に

near
chikai
近い

27. Action Words　dōsa　動作

drink
nomu　飲む

eat
taberu　食べる

sleep
nemuru　眠る

wash
arau　洗う

skate
sukēto o suru
スケートをする

fall
korobu　ころぶ

cry
naku　泣く

laugh
warau　笑う

fly
tobu　飛ぶ

write
kaku　書く

read
yomu　読む

play
(a game) **(gēmu o) suru**; (an instrument) **(gakki o) ensō suru**
（ゲームを）する　　　　　（楽器を）演奏する

sit down
suwaru　すわる

stand up
tachiagaru
立ち上がる

dance
odoru　踊る

walk
aruku　歩く

run
hashiru　走る

climb
noboru　登る

jump
tobikoeru　飛び越える

drive
unten suru　運転する

push
osu　押す

sell
uru　売る

buy
kau　買う

ski
sukii o suru
スキーをする

dive
tobikomu　飛び込む

swim
oyogu　泳ぐ

paint
(enogu de) e o kaku
（絵の具で）絵をかく

draw
(sen de) e o kaku
（線で）絵をかく

ride a bicycle
jitensha ni noru
自転車に乗る

come **kuru** 来る

go **iku** 行く

throw **nageru** 投げる

catch **ukeru** 受ける

watch **miharu** 見張る

sing **utau** 歌う

talk **hanasu** 話す

kick **keru** ける

listen (to) **kiku** 聞く

think **kangaeru** 考える

roar **hoeru** ほえる

dig **horu** 掘る

pour **mizu o yaru** 水をやる

juggle **kyokugei o suru** 曲芸をする

point (at) **. . . o sasu** …をさす

look for **sagasu** 捜す

find **mitsukeru** 見つける

give **ataeru** 与える

receive **morau** もらう

cut **kiru** 切る

cook **ryōri suru** 料理する

open **akeru** 開ける

close **shimeru** しめる

take a bath **nyūyoku suru** 入浴する

teach **oshieru** 教える

break **kowasu** こわす

fix **shūri suru** 修理する

carry **hakobu** 運ぶ

pull **hiku** 引く

wait **matsu** 待つ

28. Colors iro 色

white
shiro
白

black
kuro
黒

gray
haiiro
灰色

red
aka
赤

purple
murasaki iro
紫色

yellow
kiiro
黄色

green
midori
緑

pink
pinku
ピンク

orange
orenji iro
オレンジ色

brown
chairo
茶色

blue
aoiro
青色

gold
kin'iro
金色

silver
gin'iro
銀色

29. The Family Tree ikka no keizu 一家の系図

grandmother, grandma
sobo **obāchan**
祖母　おばあちゃん

mother, mom
haha, okāsan
母, おかあさん

father, dad
chichi, otōsan
父, おとうさん

son
musuko
むすこ

brother
ani, otōto
兄, 弟

sister
ane, imōto
姉, 妹

grandfather, grandpa
sofu **ojiichan**
祖父　おじいちゃん

uncle
oji
おじ

aunt
oba
おば

cousin
itoko
いとこ

cousin
itoko
いとこ

daughter
musume
娘

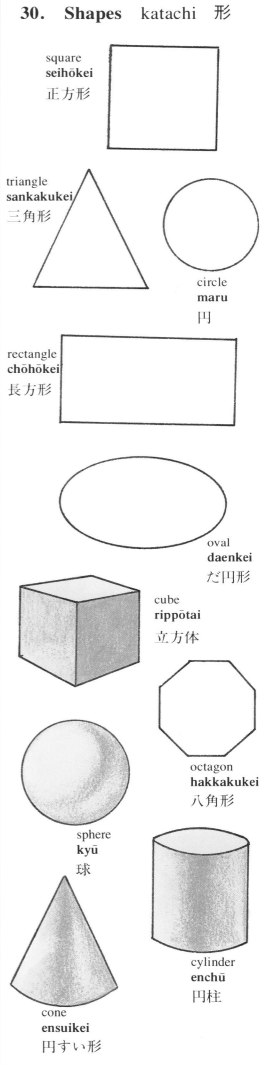

30. Shapes katachi 形

square
seihōkei
正方形

triangle
sankakukei
三角形

circle
maru
円

rectangle
chōhōkei
長方形

oval
daenkei
だ円形

cube
rippōtai
立方体

octagon
hakkakukei
八角形

sphere
kyū
球

cylinder
enchū
円柱

cone
ensuikei
円すい形

31. Numbers sū 数

Ordinal Numbers
josū
序数

tenth
jūbanme
十番目

ninth
kyūbanme
九番目

eighth
hachibanme
八番目

seventh
nanabanme,
shichibanme
七番目

sixth
rokubanme
六番目

fifth
gobanme
五番目

fourth
yonbanme
四番目

third
sanbanme
三番目

second
nibanme
二番目

first
ichibanme
一番目

Cardinal Numbers
kisu
基数

0 zero
rei
零

½ half
nibun no ichi
二分の一

1 one
ichi
一

2 two
ni
二

3 three
san
三

4 four
yon, shi
四

5 five
go
五

6 six
roku
六

16 sixteen
jūroku
十六

17 seventeen
jūnana, jūshichi
十七

18 eighteen
jūhachi
十八

19 nineteen
jūku, jūkyū
十九

20 twenty
nijū
二十

21 twenty-one
nijū-ichi
二十一

28 twenty-eight
nijū-hachi
二十八

29 twenty-nine
nijū-ku, nijū-kyū
二十九

30 thirty
sanjū
三十

31 thirty-one
sanjū-ichi
三十一

37 thirty-seven
sanjū-nana,
sanjū-shichi
三十七

38 thirty-eight
sanjū-hachi
三十八

39 thirty-nine
sanjū-ku,
sanjū-kyū
三十九

40 forty
yonjū
四十

46 forty-six
yonjū-roku
四十六

47 forty-seven
yonjū-nana, yonjū-shichi
四十七

48 forty-eight
yonjū-hachi 四十八

49 forty-nine
yonjū-ku, yonjū-kyū
四十九

55 fifty-five
gojū-go
五十五

56 fifty-six
gojū-roku
五十六

57 fifty-seven
gojū-nana,
gojū-shichi
五十七

58 fifty-eight
gojū-hachi
五十八

64 sixty-four
rokujū-yon,
rokujū-shi
六十四

65 sixty-five
rokujū-go
六十五

66 sixty-six
rokujū-roku
六十六

67 sixty-seven
rokujū-nana,
rokujū-shichi
六十七

73 seventy-three
nanajū-san, shichijū-san
七十三

74 seventy-four
nanajū-yon,
shichijū-yon
七十四

75 seventy-five
nanajū-go,
shichijū-go
七十五

76 seventy-six
nanajū-roku,
shichijū-roku
七十六

82 eighty-two
hachijū-ni
八十二

83 eighty-three
hachijū-san
八十三

84 eighty-four
hachijū-shi,
hachijū-yon
八十四

85 eighty-five
hachijū-go
八十五

91 ninety-one
kyūjū-ichi
九十一

92 ninety-two
kyūjū-ni
九十二

93 ninety-three
kyūjū-san
九十三

94 ninety-four
kyūjū-shi, kyūjū-yon
九十四

100 hundred
hyaku
百

1,000 thousand
sen
千

10,000 ten thousand
man
万

7 seven
nana, shichi
七

8 eight
hachi
八

9 nine
ku, kyū
九

10 ten
jū
十

11 eleven
jūichi
十一

12 twelve
jūni
十二

13 thirteen
jūsan
十三

14 fourteen
jūshi, jūyon
十四

15 fifteen
jūgo
十五

22 twenty-two
nijū-ni
二十二

23 twenty-three
nijū-san
二十三

24 twenty-four
nijū-shi, nijū-yon
二十四

25 twenty-five
nijū-go
二十五

26 twenty-six
nijū-roku
二十六

27 twenty-seven
nijū-nana, nijū-shichi
二十七

32 thirty-two
sanjū-ni
三十二

33 thirty-three
sanjū-san
三十三

34 thirty-four
sanjū-yon, sanjū-shi
三十四

35 thirty-five
sanjū-go
三十五

36 thirty-six
sanjū-roku
三十六

41 forty-one
yonjū-ichi
四十一

42 forty-two
yonjū-ni
四十二

43 forty-three
yonjū-san
四十三

44 forty-four
yonjū-shi, yonjū-yon
四十四

45 forty-five
yonjū-go
四十五

50 fifty
gojū
五十

51 fifty-one
gojū-ichi
五十一

52 fifty-two
gojū-ni
五十二

53 fifty-three
gojū-san
五十三

54 fifty-four
gojū-shi, gojū-yon
五十四

59 fifty-nine
gojū-ku, gojū-kyū
五十九

60 sixty
rokujū
六十

61 sixty-one
rokujū-ichi
六十一

62 sixty-two
rokujū-ni
六十二

63 sixty-three
rokujū-san
六十三

68 sixty-eight
rokujū-hachi
六十八

69 sixty-nine
rokujū-ku, rokujū-kyū
六十九

70 seventy
nanajū, shichijū
七十

71 seventy-one
nanajū-ichi, shichijū-ichi
七十一

72 seventy-two
nanajū-ni, shichijū-ni
七十二

77 seventy-seven
nanajū-nana, shichijū-shichi
七十七

78 seventy-eight
nanajū-hachi, shichijū-hachi
七十八

79 seventy-nine
nanajū-kyū, shichijū-kyū
七十九

80 eighty
hachijū
八十

81 eighty-one
hachijū-ichi
八十一

86 eighty-six
hachijū-roku
八十六

87 eighty-seven
hachijū-nana, hachijū-shichi
八十七

88 eighty-eight
hachijū-hachi
八十八

89 eighty-nine
hachijū-ku, hachijū-kyū
八十九

90 ninety
kyūjū
九十

95 ninety-five
kyūjū-go
九十五

96 ninety-six
kyūjū-roku
九十六

97 ninety-seven
kyūjū-nana, kyūjū-shichi
九十七

98 ninety-eight
kyūjū-hachi
九十八

99 ninety-nine
kyūjū-ku, kyūjū-kyū
九十九

100,000 hundred thousand
jūman
十万

1,000,000 million
hyakuman
百万

1,000,000,000 billion
jūoku
十億

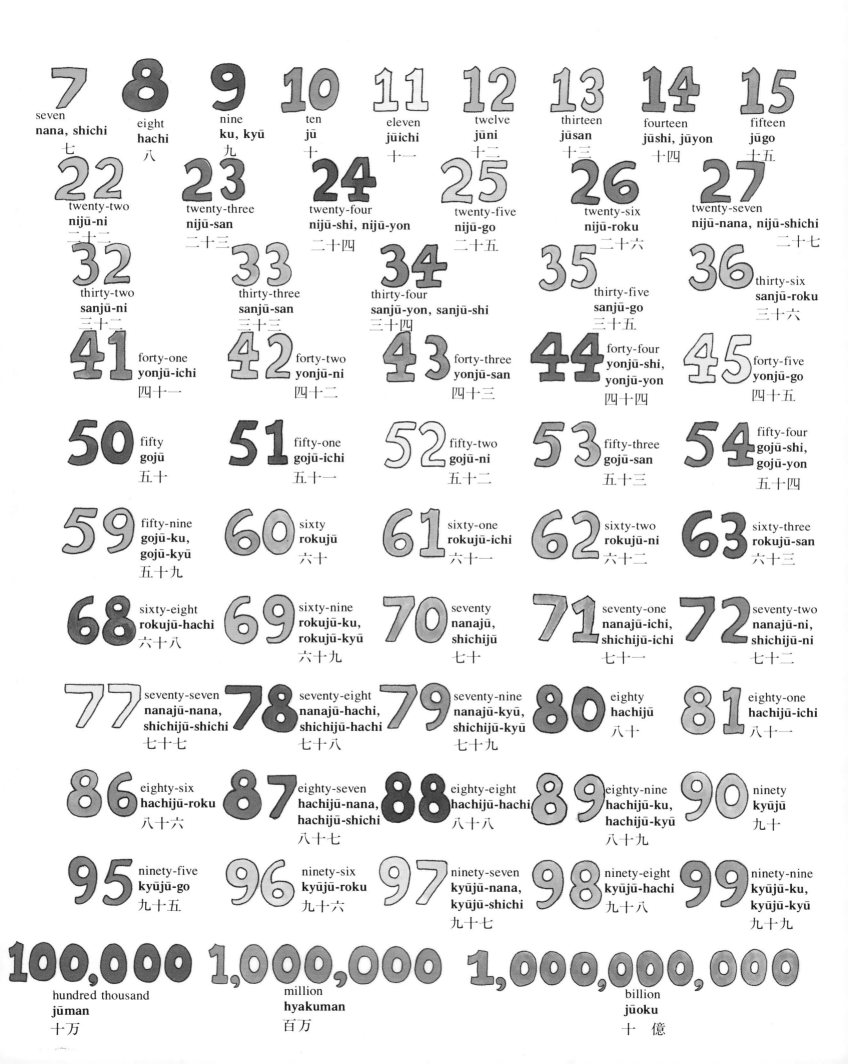

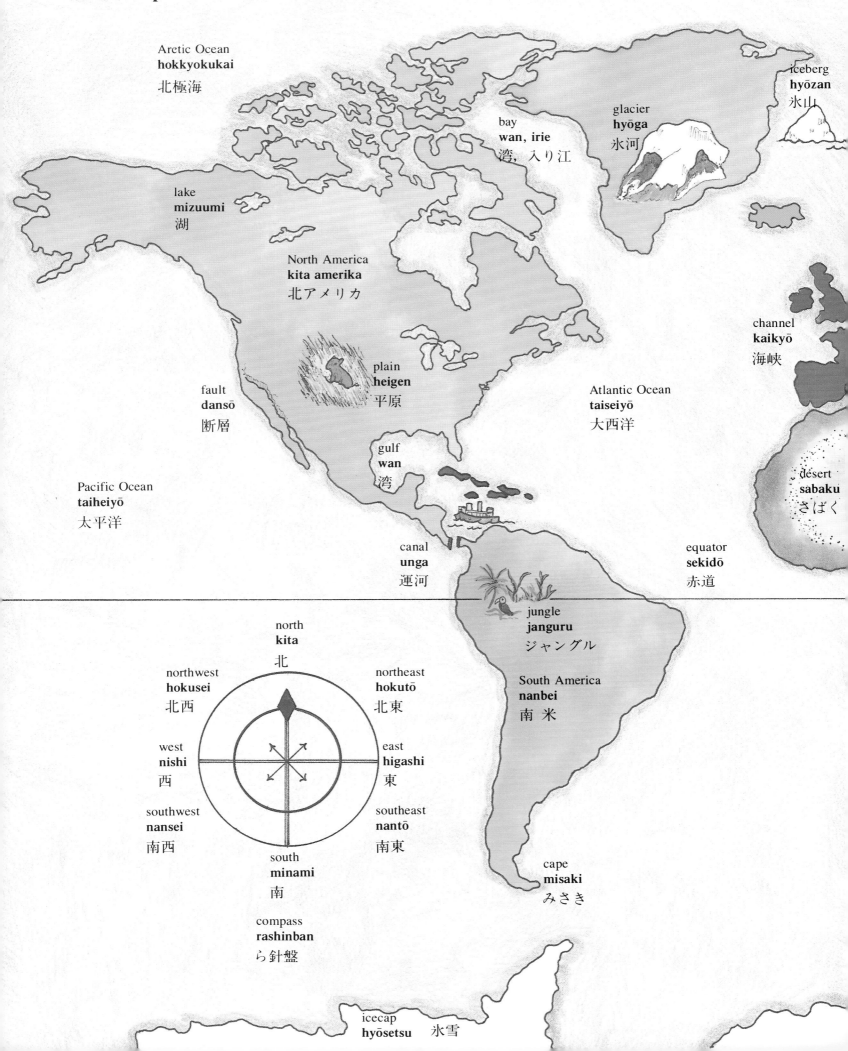

Arctic Ocean
hokkyokukai
北極海

bay
wan, irie
湾，入り江

glacier
hyōga
氷河

iceberg
hyōzan
氷山

lake
mizuumi
湖

North America
kita amerika
北アメリカ

channel
kaikyō
海峡

plain
heigen
平原

fault
dansō
断層

Atlantic Ocean
taiseiyō
大西洋

desert
sabaku
さばく

gulf
wan
湾

Pacific Ocean
taiheiyō
太平洋

canal
unga
運河

equator
sekidō
赤道

jungle
janguru
ジャングル

South America
nanbei
南米

north
kita
北

northwest
hokusei
北西

northeast
hokutō
北東

west
nishi
西

east
higashi
東

southwest
nansei
南西

southeast
nantō
南東

south
minami
南

cape
misaki
みさき

compass
rashinban
ら針盤

icecap
hyōsetsu 氷雪

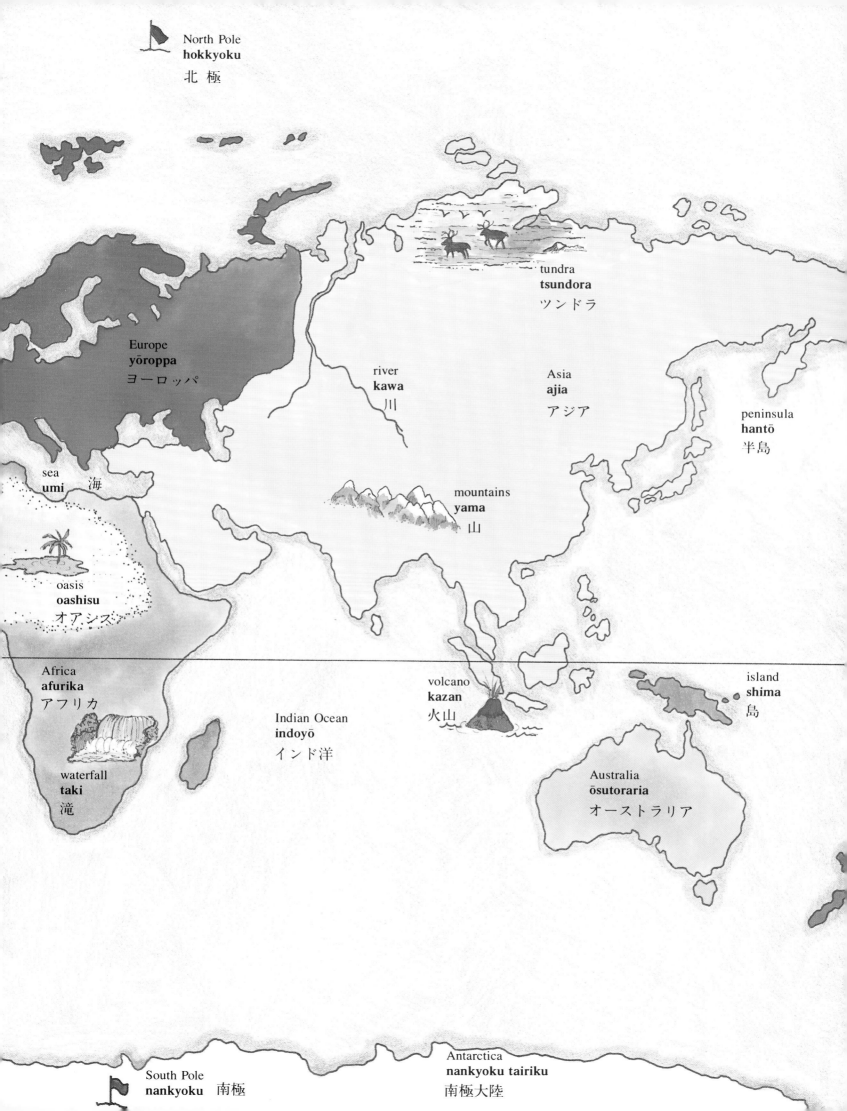

North Pole
hokkyoku
北 極

tundra
tsundora
ツンドラ

Europe
yōroppa
ヨーロッパ

river
kawa
川

Asia
ajia
アジア

peninsula
hantō
半島

sea
umi　海

mountains
yama
山

oasis
oashisu
オアシス

Africa
afurika
アフリカ

Indian Ocean
indoyō
インド洋

volcano
kazan
火山

island
shima
島

waterfall
taki
滝

Australia
ōsutoraria
オーストラリア

Antarctica
nankyoku tairiku
南極大陸

South Pole
nankyoku　南極

Japanese-English Glossary and Index

natsu, summer, 5
nattsu, nuts, 6
nawa, rope, 21
nawabashigo, rope ladder, 21
naya, barn, 9
nebukuro, sleeping bag, 9
nedan, price, 6
neji, screw, 3
nejimawashi, screwdriver, 3
nekki kyū, hot-air balloon, 16
nekkuresu, necklace, 7
neko, cat, 9
nekutai, tie, 7
nemuru, sleep, 27
nendo, clay, 24
nerihamigaki, toothpaste, 11
nēru enameru, nail polish, 12
netto, net, 18
nezumi, mouse, 9, 26; rat, 25
nezumitori, mouse hunt, 26
. . . ni mottomo chikai, next to, 26
ni, two, 31
nibanme, second, 31
nibun no ichi, half, 31
niguruma, cart, 24
niji, rainbow, 5
nijū, twenty, 31
nijū-go, twenty-five, 31
nijū-hachi, twenty-eight, 31
nijū-ichi, twenty-one, 31
nijū-ku, twenty-nine, 31
nijū-kyū, twenty-nine, 31
nijū-nana, twenty-seven, 31
nijū-ni, twenty-two, 31
nijū-roku, twenty-six, 31
nijū-san, twenty-three, 31
nijū-shi, twenty-four, 31
nijū-shichi, twenty-seven, 31
nijū-yon, twenty-four, 31
niku, meat, 6
nikuya, butcher shop, 8
nikuyasan, butcher, 15
nimotsu shitsu, cargo bay, 23
ningyō, doll, 4
ningyō no ie, dollhouse, 4
ninjin, carrots, 6
nishi, west, 32
niwa, yard, 5
nizukuriyō tēpu, packing tape, 13
. . . no aida ni, between, 26
. . . no kahō ni, down, 26
. . . no mae ni, in front of, 26
. . . no shita ni, under, 26
. . . no ue ni, above, on top of, up, 26
. . . no ushiro ni, behind, 26
noboru, climb, 27
nōfu, farmer, 9
nōjō, farm, 9
nokogiri, saw, 3
nomu, drink, 27
nōto, notebook, 1
nuno, cloth, 24
nureta, wet, 26

nurie, coloring book, 4
nyūjōken, tickets, 21
nyūjōken uriba, ticket booth, 21
nyūyoku suru, take a bath, 27

o, tail, 20
ō, king, 25
. . . o sasu, point (at), 27
oashisu, oasis, 32
oba, aunt, 29
obāchan, grandma, 29
ōbun, oven, 3
ōdan hodō, crosswalk, 16
odorite, dancer, 19
odoru, dance, 27
ohajiki, marbles, 4
oji, uncle, 29
ōji, prince, 25
ojiichan, grandpa, 29
ōjo, princess, 25
oka, hill, 9
ōkami, wolf, 20
ōkan, crown, 25
okane, money, 6
okāsan, mom, 29
ōkesutora, orchestra, 19
ōkesutora seki, orchestra pit, 19
ōkina, large, 26
okurimono, gift, 10
omocha, toys, 4
omocha no heitai, toy soldiers, 4
omochaya, toy store, 8
omoi, heavy, 26
ōmu, parrot, 20
omuretsu, omelet, 10
ondori, rooster, 9
onna, woman, 9
onna ten'in, saleswoman, 16
ono, ax, 25
orenji, orange, 6
orenji iro, orange, 28
ori, cage, 21
ōru, oar, 16
oru hito, weaver, 24
orugōru, music box, 4
osagegami, braid, 12
oshieru, teach, 27
oshiire, closet, 2
oshiroi, powder, 12
osoi, slow, 26
osu, push, 27
(osu no) kujaku, peacock, 20
ōsutoraria, Australia, 32
ōtobai, motorcycle, 16
otoko, man, 9
otōsan, dad, 29
otōto, brother, 29
oushi, bull, 9
oyayubi, thumb, 11
oyogu, swim, 27

pai, pie, 6
painappuru, pineapple, 6

pairotto, pilot, 17
pajama, pajamas, 7
pākingu mētā, parking meter, 8
pan, bread, 6
panda, panda, 20
panku shita taiya, flat tire, 14
pan'ya, bakery, 8
parashūto, parachute, 18
pasupōto, passport, 17
patokā, police car, 16
pedaru, pedal, 14
pedikyuashi, pedicurist, 12
pen, pen, 1
penchi, pliers, 14
pengin, penguin, 20
penkiya, painter, 15
pēpā taoru, paper towels, 3
piano, piano, 19
piero, clown, 21
piinatsu, peanuts, 21
pikunikku, picnic, 9
pinku, pink, 28
poketto, pocket, 7
poniitēru, ponytail, 12
poppukōn, popcorn, 21
posutā, poster, 2
pōtā, porter, 17
poteto chippu, potato chips, 6
puropera, propeller, 17
pūru, swimming pool, 18

raberu, label, 13
raimu, lime, 6
raion, lion, 20, 21
raion zukai, lion tamer, 21
rajio, radio, 2
raketto, racket, 18
rakuda, camel, 20
(rakuda no) kobu, hump, 20
ranchi, lunch, 10
rashinban, compass, 32
rēdā sukuriin, radar screen, 17
referii, referee, 18
rei, zero, 31
reitō shokuhin, frozen dinner, 6
reizōko, refrigerator, 3
rejisutā, cash register, 6
rejisutā gakari, cashier, 6
rekishi, history, 24
rekkāsha, tow truck, 14
rekōdo, record, 2
(rekōdo) purēyā, record player, 2
remon, lemon, 6
renchi, wrench, 3
renga, brick, 3
renji, stove, 3
rēnkōto, raincoat, 7
reotādo, leotard, 19
repōtā, reporter, 15
ressha, train, 16
resuringu, wrestling, 18
resutoran, restaurant, 8, 10
retasu, lettuce, 6

rihatsushi, barber, 12
rihatsuten, barber shop, 12
ringo, apple, 6
ringoame, caramel apple, 21
rippōtai, cube, 30
ro, kiln, 24
roba, donkey, 9
robotto, robot, 23
robusutā, lobster, 22
rodai, deck, 5
roketto, rocket, 23
rokkingu chea, rocking chair, 2, 4
roku, six, 31
rokubanme, sixth, 31
rokujū, sixty, 31
rokujū-go, sixty-five, 31
rokujū-hachi, sixty-eight, 31
rokujū-ichi, sixty-one, 31
rokujū-ku, sixty-nine, 31
rokujū-kyū, sixty-nine, 31
rokujū-nana, sixty-seven, 31
rokujū-ni, sixty-two, 31
rokujū-roku, sixty-six, 31
rokujū-san, sixty-three, 31
rokujū-shi, sixty-four, 31
rokujū-shichi, sixty-seven, 31
rokujū-yon, sixty-four, 31
rōpu, rope, 19
rōrā sukēto, roller skates, 16
rōsoku, candle, 10
ryōri suru, cook, 27
ryōshi, fisherman, 15
(ryōte to atama o shita ni tsukete suru) sakadachi, headstand, 21
ryū, dragon, 25
ryukkusakku, backpack, 7
ryūseiu, meteor shower, 23

sabaku, desert, 32
saboten, cactus, 1
sagasu, look for, 27
sai, rhinoceros, 20
saibankan, judge, 15
saifu, wallet, 13
saikoro, dice, 4
sain, signature, 13
sakadachi, handstand, 21
sakana, fish, 1, 10
sākasu, circus, 21
sākasu no daitento, big top, 21
sākasu no kaomise gyōretsu, circus parade, 21
sakisohon, saxophone, 19
sakkā, soccer, 18
sakkā bōru, soccer ball, 18
sakumotsu, crop, 24
sakuranbo, cherries, 6
same, shark, 22
san, three, 31
sanbanme, third, 31
sandaru, sandals, 7
sandoitchi, sandwich, 10
sango, coral, 22

sangoshō, coral reef, 22
sangurasu, sunglasses, 7
sanjū, thirty, 31
sanjū-go, thirty-five, 31
sanjū-hachi, thirty-eight, 31
sanjū-ichi, thirty-one, 31
sanjū-ku, thirty-nine, 31
sanjū-kyu, thirty-nine, 31
sanjū-nana, thirty-seven, 31
sanjū-ni, thirty-two, 31
sanjū-roku, thirty-six, 31
sanjū-san, thirty-three, 31
sanjū-shi, thirty-four, 31
sanjū-shichi, thirty-seven, 31
sanjū-yon, thirty-four, 31
sankakukei, triangle, 30
sanrinsha, tricycle, 14
sanrūfu, sunroof, 14
sanso bonbe, oxygen tank, 22
sansū no mondai, arithmetic problem, 1
sara, dishes, 3; plate, 10
sarada, salad, 10
saru, monkey, 20
sashi dashinin jūsho shimei, return address, 13
satō, sugar, 10
sayamame, green beans, 6
se, back, 11
sebiro, suit, 7
sei ga hikui, short, 26
sei no takai, tall, 26
seigyo ban, control panel, 23
seihōkei, square, 30
seiryō inryō (sui), soft drink, 10
seito, student, 1
seito no tsukue, pupil desk, 1
seiuchi, walrus, 20
seiun, nebula, 23
seiza, constellation, 23
sekai chizu, world map, 32
sekidō, equator, 32
sekiyu, oil, 14
sekken, soap, 6
sekken no awa, suds, 12
sen, thousand, 31
(sen de) e o kaku, draw, 27
senpūki, fan, 5
senro, train tracks, 9
sensei, teacher, 1
sensei no tsukue, teacher's desk, 1
senshajō, car wash, 14
sensu, fan, 4
sensuikan, submarine, 22
sentakuki, washing machine, 3
sentakumono, laundry, 3
sentakumono no kansōki, clothes dryer, 3
senzai, laundry detergent, 3
serori, celery, 10
serotēpu, cellophane tape, 1
sētā, sweater, 7
setchakuzai, glue, 1

setsuhen, snowflake, 5
setsujōsha, snowmobile, 5
shaberu, shovel, 5
shadō, driveway, 8
shanpū, shampoo, 12
sharin, wheel, 24
(sharin no) ya, spokes, 14
shashin, photograph, 4
shashu, archer, 25
shatsu, shirt, 7
shawā, shower, 2
shi, four, 31
shibakariki, lawn mower, 5
shichi, seven, 31
shichibanme, seventh, 31
shichijū, seventy, 31
shichijū-go, seventy-five, 31
shichijū-hachi, seventy-eight, 31
shichijū-ichi, seventy-one, 31
shichijū-kyū, seventy-nine, 31
shichijū-ni, seventy-two, 31
shichijū-roku, seventy-six, 31
shichijū-san, seventy-three, 31
shichijū-shichi, seventy-seven, 31
shichijū-yon, seventy-four, 31
shida, fern, 24
shihei, bill, 13
shii-dii, compact disc, 2
shiiku gakari, zookeeper, 20
shiiriaru, cereal, 6
shiisō, seesaw, 8
shiito beruto, seat belt, 14
shiitsu, sheet, 2
shika, deer, 20
shika eisei gishi, dental hygienist, 11
shikaiin, dentist's office, 11
shikaisha, master of ceremonies, 19
shikenkan, test tube, 23
shiki, four seasons, 5
shikimono, rug, 1
shikisha, conductor, 19
shima, island, 32; stripes, 20
shimauma, zebra, 20
shimegane, buckle, 7
shimeru, close, 27
shinbaru, cymbals, 19
shinbun, newspaper, 8
shinsatsudai, examining table, 11
shinshitsu, bedroom, 2
shio, salt, 10
shiretsu kyōseigu, braces, 11
shiro, castle, 25; white, 28
shirokuma, polar bear, 20
shiruku hatto, top hat, 4
shisho, librarian, 15
shishobako, post-office box, 13
shita, tongue, 11
shitagi, underwear, 7
shōbōsha, fire engine, 16
shōbōshi, fire fighter, 15
shōbōsho, fire station, 8
shōgai kyōsō, hurdles, 18
shōjo, girl, 9

English-Japanese Glossary and Index

candle, rōsoku, 10
candy, kyandē, 6
cane, tsue, 11
cannon, taihō, 22
canoe, kanū, 16
cap, kyappu, 7
cape, katamanto, 21; misaki, 32
car, jidōsha, 16
car racing, kā rēsu, 18
car wash, senshajō, 14
caramel apple, ringoame, 21
cardinal numbers, kisū, 31
cards, toranpu, 4
cargo bay, nimotsu shitsu, 23
carpenter, daiku, 15
carpet, jūtan, kāpetto, 2
carrots, ninjin, 6
carry, hakobu, 27
cart, niguruma, 24
cartwheel, yoko tonbogaeri, 21
cash register, rejisutā, 6
cashier, rejisutā gakari, 6
cassette player, kasetto dekki, 2
cassette tape, kasetto tēpu, 2
cast, gipusu, 11
castle, shiro, 25
cat, neko, 9
catch, ukeru, 27
cave, hora ana, 24
cave drawing, hora ana kaiga, 24
cave dwellers, ana kyojin, 24
ceiling, tenjō, 2
celery, serori, 10
cello, chero, 19
cellophane tape, serotēpu, 1
cement mixer, konkuriito mikisā, 16
cereal, kokumotsu shoku, shiiriaru, 6
chain mail, kusari yoroi, 25
chair, isu, 3
chalk, chōku, 1
chalkboard, kokuban, 1
channel, kaikyō, 32
check, kogitte, 13
checkbook, kogittechō, 13
checkers, chekkā, 4
cheek, hoho, 11
cheese, chiizu, 6
cherries, sakuranbo, 6
chess, chesu, 4
chest, mune, 11
chick, hiyoko, 9
chicken, chikin, toriniku, 10
children, kodomo, 19
chimney, entotsu, 2
chin, ago, 11
chocolate, chokorēto, 6
church, kyōkai, 8
circle, en, maru, 30
circus, sākasu, 21
circus parade, sākasu no kaomise gyōretsu, 21
city, toshi, 8
clam, hamaguri, 22
clarinet, kurarinetto, 19
classroom, kyōshitsu, 1
claws, tsume, 20
clay, nendo, 24
clean, kirei na, 26
climb, noboru, 27
clock, tokei, 1

close, shimeru, 27
closed, tojita, 26
closet, oshiire, 2
cloth, nuno, 24
clothes dryer, sentakumono no kansōki, 3
clothing, mi ni tsukeru mono, 7
clothing store, yōfukuya, 8
clouds, kumo, 5
clown, piero, 21
club, konbō, 24
coat, uwagi, 7
cobweb, kumo no su, 4
coffee, kōhii, 10
coin, kōka, 13
cold, tsumetai, 26
collar, karā, eri, 7
colored pencils, iroenpitsu, 1
coloring book, nurie, 4
colors, iro, 28
colt, kouma, 9
comb, kushi, 12
come, kuru, 27
comet, suisei, 23
comic books, mangabon, 4
community, chiiki, 15
compact disc, shii-dii, 2
compass, konpasu, 1; rashinban, 32
computer programmer, conpyūtā no puroguramā, 15
computer, konpyūtā, 23
concorde, konkorudo, 17
conductor, shikisha, 19
cone, ensuikei, 30
constellation, seiza, 23
construction worker, kensetsu sagyōin, 15
control panel, seigyo ban, 23
control tower, kansei tō, 17
cook, kokku, 15; ryōri suru, 27
cookies, kukkii, 6
copilot, fuku pairotto, 17
coral, sango, 22
coral reef, sangoshō, 22
corn, tōmorokoshi, 24
corner, kado, magarikado, machikado, 8
costume, ishō, 19
cotton candy, watagashi, 21
counter, kauntā, 3
country, inaka, 9
court jester, kyūtei dōkeshi, 25
courtyard, nakaniwa, 25
cousin, itoko, 29
coveralls, tsunagi, kabārōru, 14
cow, meushi, 9
cowboy, kaubōi, 15
cowboy boots, kaubōi būtsu, 4
cowboy hat, kaubōi hatto, 4
crab, kani, 22
crackers, bisuketto, kurakkā, 6
cradle, yurikago, 4
crane, kurēn, 8
crater, kurētā, 23
crayon, kureyon, 1
cream, kuriimu, 10
credit card, kurejitto kādo, 13
crew cut, kakugari, 12
crop, sakumotsu, 24
cross-country skiing, kurosu-kantorii

sukii, 18
crosswalk, ōdan hodō, 16
crown, ōkan, 25
cruise ship, yūransen, 16
crutch, matsubazue, 11
cry, naku, 27
cube, rippōtai, 30
cup, kappu, chawan, 10
curlers, kārā, 12
curling iron, hea airon, 12
curly, kāru shita, 12
curtain, maku, 19
curtains, kāten, 2
customs officer, zeikanri, 17
cut, kiru, 27
cycling, jitensha kyōsō, 18
cylinder, enchū, 30
cymbals, shinbaru, 19

dad, otōsan, 29
dance, odoru, 27
dancer, odorite, 19
dark, (iro ga) koi, 26
dashboard, dasshubōdo, 14
daughter, musume, 29
deck, barukonii, rodai, 5
deer, shika, 20
dental floss, itoyōji, 11
dental hygienist, shika eisei gishi, 11
dentist, haisha, 11
dentist's office, shikaiin, 11
desert, sabaku, 32
desk, tsukue, 1
dice, saikoro, 4
difficult, muzukashii, 26
dig, horu, 27
dining room, dainingu rūmu, 2
dinner, yūshoku, dinā, 10
dinosaur, kyōryū, 24
dirt, gomi, 9
dirty, kitanai, 26
disc jockey, disuku jokkii, 15
dishes, sara, 3
dishwasher, (jidō) sara araiki, 3
dive, tobikomu, 27
diving, tobikomi, 18
dock, funatsukiba, 16
doctor, isha, 11
doctor's office, iin, 11
dog, inu, 9
doll, ningyō, 4
dollhouse, ningyō no ie, 4
dolphin, iruka, 22
donkey, roba, 9
door, doa, 2
door handle, doa no totte, 14
doorman, doaman, 15
down, . . . no kahō ni, 26
down vest, chokki, besuto, 7
downhill skiing, kakkō kyōgi, 18
dragon, ryū, 25
draw, (sen de) e o kaku, 27
drawbridge, hanebashi, 25
drawer, hikidashi, 3
dress, fuku, doresu, 7
dresser, doressā, (kyōdaitsuki) keshōdansu, 2
dressing room, gakuya, 19
drill, doriru, 3
drink, nomu, 27

drive, unten suru, 27
drive-in, doraibuin ginkō, 13
driver's seat, untenseki, 14
driveway, shadō, 8
drugstore, yakkyoku, 8
drum, doramu, 19
dry, kawaita, 26
duck, ahiru, 9
duckling, ahiru no ko, 9
dull, kireaji no nibui, 26
dungeon, chikarō, 25
dust, hokori, chiri, 4
dustpan, chiritori, 3

eagle, washi, 20
ear, mimi, 11
earmuffs, mimiate, 7
earring, iyaringu, 7
earth, chikyū, 23
easel, gaka, 1
east, higashi, 32
easy, yasashii, 26
eat, taberu, 27
eggs, tamago, 6
eight, hachi, 31
eighteen, jūhachi, 31
eighth, hachibanme, 31
eighty, hachijū, 31
eighty-eight, hachijū-hachi, 31
eighty-five, hachijū-go, 31
eighty-four, hachijū-shi, hachijū-yon, 31
eighty-nine, hachijū-ku, hachijū-kyū, 31
eighty-one, hachijū-ichi, 31
eighty-seven, hachijū-nana, hachijū-shichi, 31
eighty-six, hachijū-roku, 31
eighty-three, hachijū-san, 31
eighty-two, hachijū-ni, 31
elbow, hiji, 11
electric mixer, mikisā, 3
electric train, denki kikansha, 4
electrical outlet, konsento, 3
electrician, denkikō, 15
elephant, zō, 20, 21
elevator, erebētā, 17
eleven, jūichi, 31
elf, shōyōsei, 25
empty, kara no, 26
engine, enjin, 14, 17
equator, sekidō, 32
eraser, kokubanfuki, 1; keshigomu, 1
escalator, esukarētā, 17
europe, yōroppa, 32
examining table, shinsatsudai, 11
eyebrow, mayu, 11
eyes, me, 11

face, kao, 11
factory, kōba, 8
factory worker, kōin, 15
fairy, yōsei, 25
fall, aki, 5; korobu, 27
family tree, ikka no keizu, 29
fan, sensu, 4, senpūki, 5
far, tōi, 26
farm, nōjō, 9
farmer, nōfu, 9
fashion designer, fasshon dezainā, 15

fast, hayai, 26
fat, futotta, 26
father, chichi, 29
faucet, jaguchi, kokku, 3
fault, dansō, 32
feather, hane, 4
feathers, umō, 20
fence, kakoi, 9
fender, fendā, doroyoke, 14
fern, shida, 24
field, hatake, 24
fifteen, jūgo, 31
fifth, gobanme, 31
fifty, gojū, 31
fifty-eight, gojū-hachi, 31
fifty-five, gojū-go, 31
fifty-four, gojū-shi, gojū-yon, 31
fifty-nine, gojū-ku, gojū-kyū, 31
fifty-one, gojū-ichi, 31
fifty-seven, gojū-nana, gojū-shichi, 31
fifty-six, gojū-roku, 31
fifty-three, gojū-san, 31
fifty-two, gojū-ni, 31
file, yasuri, 3
file cabinet, shorui dana, 13
film, firumu, 21
fin, hire, 22
find, mitsukeru, 27
finger, yubi, 11
fingernail, yubi no tsume, 12
fire, hi, 24
fire engine, shōbōsha, 16
fire escape, hijō kaidan, 8
fire fighter, shōbōshi, 15
fire hydrant, shōkasen, 8
fire station, shōbōsho, 8
fireplace, danro, 2
first, ichibanme, 31
fish, sakana, 1, 10
fisherman, ryōshi, 15
fishhook, tsuribari, 22
fishing, tsuri, gyorō, 24
fishing line, tsuri ito, 22
five, go, 31
fix, shūri suru, 27
flags, hata, 17
flamingo, furamingo, 20
flashbulb, sutorobo, 21
flashlight, kaichū dentō, 3
flat tire, panku shita taiya, 14
flight attendant, jōkyaku gakari, 17
flint, hiuchi ishi, 24
flipper, ashihire, 22
floor, yuka, 2
florist, hanaya, 15
flour, komugiko, 3
flowerbed, kadan, 5
flowers, hana, 5
flute, furūto, 19
fly, hae, 5; tobu, 27
fly swatter, haetataki, 5
fog, kiri, 5
food, shokumotsu, 6
food processor, fūdo purosessā (bannō chōri yōgu), 3
foot, ashi, 11
football, (futtobōru no) bōru, amerikan futtobōru, 18
footprint, ashiato, 23
footstool, sutsūru, 2

forehead, hitai, 11
foreman, genba kantoku, 15
forest, mori, 25
forge, kajiba no ro, 25
fork, fōku, 10
forty, yonjū, 31
forty-eight, yonjū-hachi, 31
forty-five, yonjū-go, 31
forty-four, yonjū-shi, yonjū-yon, 31
forty-nine, yonjū-ku, yonjū-kyū, 31
forty-one, yonjū-ichi, 31
forty-seven, yonjū-nana, yonjū-shichi, 31
forty-six, yonjū-roku, 31
forty-three, yonjū-san, 31
forty-two, yonjū-ni, 31
fountain, funsui, 8
four, yon, shi, 31
four seasons, shiki, 5
fourteen, jūshi, jūyon, 31
fourth, yonbanme, 31
fox, kitsune, 20
freckles, sobakasu, 12
freezer, furiizā, 3
french fries, furenchi poteto, 10
french horn, furenchi horun, 19
frog, kaeru, 9
frozen dinner, reitō shokuhin, 6
fruit, kudamono, 6
fruit juice, furūtsu jūsu, 6
full, ippai no, 26
fur, kegawa, 24

galaxy, gingakei, 23
game, gēmu, gēmuban, 4
garage, garēji, 14
garden hose, mizumaki hōsu, 5
gardener, uekiya, 15
garment bag, ishōire kaban, 17
gas cap, gasorin no futa, 14
gas pump, gasorin ponpu, 14
gas station, gasorin sutando, 14
gate, gēto, 17
giant, kyojin, 25
gift, okurimono, 10
gills, era, 22
giraffe, kirin, 20
girl, shōjo, 9
give, ataeru, 27
glacier, hyōga, 32
glass, koppu, gurasu, 10
glasses, megane, 7
globe, chikyūgi, 1
gloves, tebukuro, 7
glue, setchakuzai, 1
go, iku, 27
go!, susume, 16
goat, yagi, 9
goggles, gōguru, 18
gold, kinka, 22; kin'iro, 28
golf, gorufu, 18
golf club, gorufu kurabu, 18
good, yoi, 26
goose, gachō, 9
gorilla, gorira, 20
gosling, gachō no hina, 9
grandfather, sofu, 29
grandma, obāchan, 29
grandmother, sobo, 29
grandpa, ojiichan, 29

pupil desk, seito no tsukue, 1
puppet, yubi ningyō, 4
puppy, koinu, 9
purple, murasaki iro, 28
purse, handobaggu, 17
push, osu, 27

queen, joō, 25
quiver, yazutsu, 25

rabbit, usagi, 9
race car, kyōsōyō no kuruma, 14
racket, raketto, 18
radar screen, rēdā sukuriin, 17
radio, rajio, 2
rag, borokire, 14
rain, ame, 5
rainbow, niji, 5
raincoat, rēnkōto, 7
raindrop, amadare, 5
rake, kumade, 5
raspberries, kiichigo, 6
rat, nezumi, 25
razor, kamisori, 12
read, yomu, 27
rearview mirror, bakku mirā, 14
receive, morau, 27
receptionist, uketsuke gakari, 13
record, rekōdo, 2
record player, (rekōdo) purēyā, 2
rectangle, chōhōkei, 30
red, akai, 12; aka, 28
referee, referii, 18
reflectors, hanshakyō, 14
refrigerator, reizōko, 3
reins, tazuna, 25
reporter, repōtā, 15
rest rooms, toire, 21
restaurant, resutoran, 8, 10
return address, sashi dashinin jūsho shimei, 13
rhinoceros, sai, 20
rice, gohan, 10
ride a bicycle, jitensha ni noru, 27
right, migi no, 26
ring, yubiwa, 7; wa, 21
ringmaster, engi kantoku, 21
rings, (wakusei no) wa, 23
river, kawa, 32
road, dōro, 9
roar, hoeru, 27
robot, robotto, 23
rock, iwa, 24
rocket, roketto, 23
rocking chair, rokkingu chea, 2, 4
rocking horse, yuri mokuba, 4
roller skates, rōrā sukēto, 16
roof, yane, 2
rooster, ondori, 9
rope, rōpu, 19; nawa, 21
rope ladder, nawabashigo, 21
rowboat, bōto, 16
rubber band, wagomu, 13
rubber stamp, gomuin, 13
rug, shikimono, 1
ruler, jōgi, 1
run, hashiru, 27
running, kyōsō, 18
runway, kassōro, 17

saber-toothed tiger, kenshi tora, 24
sad, kanashii, 26
saddle, kura, 25
safe, kinko, 13
safety deposit box, kashi kinko, 13
safety net, anzen netto, 21
sail, ho, 16
sailboat, hansen, 16
sailing, yotto, 18
sailor, suihei, 15
salad, sarada, 10
salesman, danshi ten'in, 15
saleswoman, onna ten'in, joshi ten'in, 16
salt, shio, 10
sand, sunahama, 22
sandals, sandaru, 7
sandbox, sunaba, 8
sandpaper, kamiyasuri, 3
sandwich, sandoitchi, 10
satellite, jinkō eisei, 23
saucer, ukezara, 10
sausages, sōsēji, 10
saw, nokogiri, 3
saxophone, sakisohon, 19
scale, hakari, 6, 13
scales, uroko, 22
scarf, erimaki, 7
scenery, (butai no) haikei, 19
school, gakkō, 8
school bus, sukūru basu, 16
school (of fish), mure, 22
scientist, kagakusha, 23
scissors, hasami, 1, 12
scooter, kata ashi sukēto, 16
screw, neji, 3
screwdriver, nejimawashi, 3
script, daihon, 19
scuba diver, sukyuba daibā, 22
sea, umi, 32
sea horse, tatsu no otoshigo, 22
sea turtle, umigame, 22
sea urchin, uni, 22
seal, azarashi, 20
seashell, kai, 22
seasons, kisetsu, 5
seat, zaseki, 17
seat belt, shiito beruto, 14
seaweed, kaisō, 22
second, nibanme, 31
secretary, hisho, 15
security camera, bōhan kamera, 13
security guard, keibiin, 13
seesaw, shiisō, 8
sell, uru, 27
seven, nana, shichi, 31
seventeen, jūnana, jūshichi, 31
seventh, nanabanme, shichibanme, 31
seventy, nanajū, shichijū, 31
seventy-eight, nanajū-hachi, shichijū-hachi, 31
seventy-five, nanajū-go, shichijū-go, 31
seventy-four, nanajū-yon, shichijū-yon, 31
seventy-nine, nanajū-ku, shichijū-kyū, 31
seventy-one, nanajū-ichi, shichijū-ichi, 31
seventy-seven, nanajū-nana,

shichijū-shichi, 31
seventy-six, nanajū-roku, shichijū-roku, 31
seventy-three, nanajū-san, shichijū-san, 31
seventy-two, nanajū-ni, shichijū-ni, 31
sewing machine, mishin, 19
shadow, kage, 9
shampoo, shanpū, 12
shapes, katachi, 30
shark, same, fuka, 22
sharp, surudoi, 26
shaving cream, higesoriyō kuriimu, 12
sheep, hitsuji, 9
sheet, shiitsu, 2
sheet music, gakufu, 19
shelf, tana, 2
shield, tate, 25
shipwreck, nanpasen, 22
shirt, shatsu, 7
shoelace, kutsuhimo, 7
shoes, kutsu, 7
shopping bag, kaimono bukuro, 6
shopping cart, kaimono guruma, 6
short, mijikai, 12, sei ga hikui, 26
shorts, hanzubon, 7
shoulder, kata, 11
shovel, shaberu, 5
shower, shawā, 2
sidewalk, hodō, 16
sign, hyōshiki, hyōji, 6; kanban, 8
signature, sain, 13
silver, ginka, 22; gin'iro, 28
sing, utau, 27
singer, kashu, 19
sink, (daidokoro no) nagashi, 3
sister, ane, imōto, 29
sit down, suwaru, 27
six, roku, 31
sixteen, jūroku, 31
sixth, rokubanme, 31
sixty, rokujū, 31
sixty-eight, rokujū-hachi, 31
sixty-five, rokujū-go, 31
sixty-four, rokujū-yon, rokujū-shi, 31
sixty-nine, rokujū-ku, rokujū-kyū, 31
sixty-one, rokujū-ichi, 31
sixty-seven, rokujū-nana, rokujū-shichi, 31
sixty-six, rokujū-roku, 31
sixty-three, rokujū-san, 31
sixty-two, rokujū-ni, 31
skate, sukēto o suru, 27
skateboard, sukētobōdo, 16
skates, sukēto gutsu, 18
skating, sukēto, 18
skeleton, kokkaku, 24
ski, sukii o suru, 27
skirt, sukāto, 7
skis, sukii, 18
sky, sora, 9
skydiving, sukaidaibingu, 18
skyscraper, chōkōsō biru, 8
sled, sori, 5
sleep, nemuru, 27
sleeping bag, nebukuro, 9
sleeve, sode, 7
slide, suberidai, 8
sling, tsuri hōtai, 11
slow, osoi, 26